ESSENTIAL
BRITISH
HISTORY

Antonia Cunningham

Illustrated by Stephen Conlin and
Gerald Wood

Designed by Radhi Parekh

Consultants: Anne Millard, Peter McDonough, Alan Midgley
and Simon Rockell
Series editor: Jane Chisholm
With thanks to Anthony Marks

Contents

About this book

This book is a survey of the most important political, social and economic events in British history from the Stone Age to modern times. The main body of the book is divided into six sections which for easy reference are colour coded as follows:

Early Britain: from Stone Age times to the end of the Anglo-Saxon period (15,000BC-AD1066)

The Middle Ages: from the Norman invasion (1066) to the death of the last Plantagenet king (1487)

The Tudors and Stuarts: from the first Tudor monarch to the end of the 17th century

The 18th century

The 19th century

The 20th century

This is followed by a reference section. The 'Who's who' on pages 51-53 deals with the lives and achievements of important artistic and literary figures. There is a glossary on pages 54-56 of words and phrases that may need more explanation. On page 57 there is a list of major technological changes in Britain since the 15th century. On pages 58-59 there are lists of Britain's kings, queens and Prime Ministers. This is followed by an index on page 60.

Foreign or unfamiliar words are written in italic type. Words that appear in the glossary are also written in italic type and are followed by an asterisk *, like this: *annex**.

Dates

Many early dates begin with the abbreviation **c.** This stands for *circa*, the Latin word for 'about'. It is used when historians are unsure exactly when an event took place.

Dates shown with the letters BC refer to the period before the birth of Jesus Christ. AD stands for *Anno Domini*, which is Latin for 'Year of our Lord'. It applies to the years after the birth of Jesus Christ.

Dates after the names of kings and queens tell you the length of their reigns. Dates given after the names of politicians refer to their periods of office.

On most pages of this book there are charts which summarize the events of that particular period. They will help you to remember important events and dates.

Britain and British history

This book is chiefly concerned with events in the history of Great Britain. The word Britain derives from *Britannia*, the name given by the Romans to the area which is now England, Scotland and Wales. When the Romans arrived in Britain in AD43, the country was made up of many smaller communities, each ruled by a local king or chief. These gradually came under the control of one ruler.

By 1603 one king ruled Scotland, Wales and England, and the island became known as Great Britain. In 1801 Ireland also officially came under British rule and England, Wales, Scotland and Ireland became known collectively as the United Kingdom of Great Britain and Ireland. In 1937 Southern Ireland was established as Eire, an independent *sovereign** state. The United Kingdom became known as the United Kingdom of Great Britain and Northern Ireland.

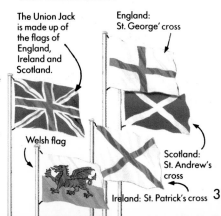

The Union Jack is made up of the flags of England, Ireland and Scotland.

England: St. George' cross

Welsh flag

Scotland: St. Andrew's cross

Ireland: St. Patrick's cross

3

Early Britain

The Stone Age

The first evidence in Britain of human life (*Homo sapiens sapiens*) dates from about 15,000BC. These early people lived in caves, hunting animals and gathering plants. They made tools and weapons out of flint and bone. This is known as the Palaeolithic era, or Old Stone Age. During this period, northern Europe was covered in ice. In about 8500BC the climate began to improve.

In about 4000BC an early farming people began arriving in Britain from mainland Europe, and by 3500BC farming had largely superseded hunting. Land was cleared to graze animals and grow food and people began to build huts of stone or wood. This is called the Neolithic era, or New Stone Age.

Stonehenge

Henges (stone or wooden circles) were first built around 2500BC, perhaps for sacred rites involving the sun. At Stonehenge (c.2305BC-1540BC) the stones align with the position of the sun at certain times of year.

Religious beliefs

It is thought that Neolithic and Bronze Age people worshipped gods connected with nature. These people believed in life after death, burying their dead with food and belongings in long or round communal tombs called barrows. Many graves dating from about 2750BC contain 'bell beakers', a style of pot made in mainland Europe. This suggests that a new people came to Britain from further east or that Britons traded abroad.

After about 1500BC people were often cremated. Iron Age people (see opposite) believed their gods lived in natural places – in forests, on hilltops or by water. Their priests, known as druids, were an important part of society. They made human and animal sacrifices to the gods.

Bell beaker

The Bronze Age

Bronze, made by mixing copper with tin, was in use in Britain from about 2100BC. It gives a sharp cutting edge and is very solid, so its discovery enabled metalsmiths to make better weapons, tools and utensils.

A typical Bronze Age farm   Storage hut

Walls were made of interwoven twigs covered with mud. (This is called wattle and daub.)

Roofs were made of thatch or turf.

By about 1200BC people were living in small, self-sufficient villages made up of a few families. Each one may have belonged to a larger community ruled by a chief. Archaeological evidence shows that from around 1000BC fortified settlements were being built. This suggests that warfare was more common.

The Iron Age

The technique of *smelting** iron, first used in mainland Europe, had reached Britain by about 700BC. It may have been brought by the first of the *Celts** who came from Europe and settled in Britain between about 500BC and 50BC.

Dagger

Iron Age pots

During the Iron Age people belonged to tribes ruled by chiefs. They lived in villages or on farms, although later there were also some larger settlements known as *oppida*. Hill forts were built in southern England from about 500BC. In peacetime they may have been trading and administrative centres; in wartime they protected people and cattle.

Trade existed with mainland Europe. By the 1st century AD foreign coins were introduced and British metalsmiths began making their own.

Roman Britain

The Romans were a people from central Italy who conquered a huge empire in Europe, the Middle East and Africa. Led by a general called Julius Caesar, Roman troops invaded the south of Britain in 55BC and again the following year. The local tribes resisted Roman attack but eventually submitted and agreed to pay *tributes** to Rome.

The Roman empire, AD100

The Romans returned in AD43 and by AD47 they had occupied an area stretching north as far as the Severn and Trent rivers. They set up their own administrative systems, but gave day-to-day control to loyal local tribes.

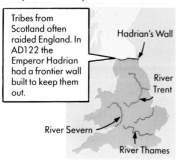

Tribes from Scotland often raided England. In AD122 the Emperor Hadrian had a frontier wall built to keep them out.

Hadrian's Wall

River Trent

River Severn

River Thames

Roman territory in Britain, AD406

A typical Romano-British town

Boudicca's revolt

Boudicca, queen of a British tribe, the Iceni, led an uprising against a tyrannical Roman governor in AD61. Although she was successful at first, the Romans eventually suppressed the revolt and Boudicca committed suicide.

Over the next 50 years, the Romans extended control over the rest of England and Wales but Caledonia (Scotland) remained hostile and unconquered. The Romans never tried to conquer Ireland.

The Roman legacy

The Romans brought writing and a sophisticated legal system into Britain. They introduced the alphabet we use today, and almost half the words in modern English derive from Latin, the language the Romans spoke. They created new towns (some with up to 50,000 people), and introduced proper drainage systems, houses with glass windows, and a form of central heating. Long straight roads were built which stretched to Scotland, Wales and Cornwall. In this way internal trade and communications were improved. The Romans also encouraged trade across the empire.

The Romans introduced new types of food and flowers into Britain.

The Romans withdrew their troops from Britain in AD410 because the army was needed to prevent *barbarian** invasions in mainland Europe. Once the Romans had departed, the civilization they left behind gradually fell into decay.

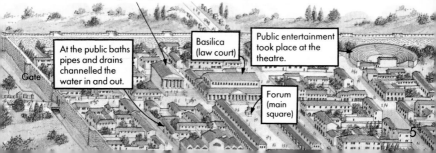

Temple to Jupiter, king of the gods.

At the public baths pipes and drains channelled the water in and out.

Gate

Basilica (law court)

Public entertainment took place at the theatre.

Forum (main square)

Britain in Anglo-Saxon times

In the 5th century Britain was invaded by *Angles**, *Saxons** and *Jutes** who came from northern Europe. By AD600 the Anglo-Saxons (as they became known) occupied most of England. Many native Britons escaped the invasions and fled to Wales, Scotland, Cornwall and Ireland.

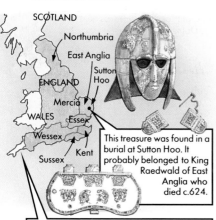

SCOTLAND
Northumbria
East Anglia
Sutton Hoo
ENGLAND
Mercia
WALES Essex
Wessex
Sussex Kent

This treasure was found in a burial at Sutton Hoo. It probably belonged to King Raedwald of East Anglia who died c.624.

The legendary King Arthur of Camelot may have been a 6th century British chief who lived in the west of Britain.

By the 7th century England consisted of seven kingdoms which competed for supremacy. The strong kingdoms often controlled their weaker neighbours. In the 7th century Northumbria was the strongest but Mercia then became dominant under King Offa (757-96). Offa was the first to call himself 'King of the English'. Later, in the 9th century, Wessex became dominant under King Alfred the Great (871-99).

Anglo-Saxon society

At first the Anglo-Saxons lived in small farming communities, but in the 7th century towns began to appear and trade increased. Saxon kings were supported by warrior nobles called *thegns* (pronounced 'thanes'). Most of the population were free peasants, but there were also some slaves, many of whom were originally native Britons. The Anglo-Saxon word for 'slave' was *wealh*. It originally meant 'Briton' and is the word from which 'Wales' derives.

In the 8th century money was minted for the first time since the Roman occupation.

Anglo-Saxon society was based on bonds of loyalty to the family and the local lord. The first written laws, set down in the 6th century, depended on this principle. In Alfred's reign this became more formalized. *Thegns* were obliged to provide him with a number of trained warriors. The number related to the amount of land they owned.

Government

Most major decisions were made by the king and his council of advisers. Local decisions were made by the local *thegn*. Alfred's council in Wessex, called the Witan, consisted of both *thegns* and churchmen.

By 900 England was organized into areas called shires or counties. Each was controlled by a *shire reeve* (sheriff). He collected taxes, organized local legal matters and enforced law and order.

King Alfred

Alfred of Wessex saved England from conquest by the Vikings (see opposite). He established a strong army, constructed fortresses along the south coast and built up a fleet of ships. He also built fortified towns called *burghs* which became thriving trading centres.

Alfred sought to revive learning, which had declined during the Viking invasions. He invited craftsmen and

scholars to his court and insisted that the clergy should learn Latin properly as this was the language of the Church. He also encouraged his nobles to learn to read and write English. The *Anglo-Saxon Chronicle*, a yearly account of events, was probably begun during his reign.

This jewel may have belonged to Alfred. The inscription says 'Alfred ordered me to be made'.

Scotland

Scotland had not been conquered by the Romans, but its native inhabitants, the *Picts**, had to combat sea raiders from Ireland and Scandinavia (see below).

Scotland takes its name from the Scots, an Irish tribe who first settled there at the start of the 6th century. They founded the kingdom of Dalriada and gradually extended control. The King of the Scots, Kenneth MacAlpin (see page 14), became King of all Scotland in 843 after the last Pictish king, Eoghann, died fighting the Vikings.

The Viking invasions

A Viking ship

The Vikings, seafarers from Scandinavia, attacked northern Europe in the 8th century. Danish Vikings reached Britain in 789 and Ireland in 795 (see page 15). By 871 they controlled East Anglia, Northumbria, York and Mercia. They advanced into Wessex too, but King Alfred defeated them at the Battle of Edington in 878. He made the Danes accept *Christianity**, and allowed them to live in a part of eastern England which became known as the Danelaw. In 886 he captured London and was accepted as king everywhere except the Danelaw.

Alfred's grandson Athelstan (925-39) seized the Danelaw in 926. The country was ruled by the Anglo-Saxons until 1013 when, after repeated Viking invasions, they surrendered to King Sweyn of Denmark. The Anglo-Saxon king, Ethelred the Unready†, (978-1016), fled to Normandy. Sweyn's son Canute became king (1016-35). However, when the Danish royal line died out in 1042, Ethelred's son Edward became king. He was known as 'the Confessor', because of his piety. Edward married the Earl of Wessex's daughter but had no children. When he died in 1066, three men claimed the throne: William, Duke of Normandy, Harold, Earl of Wessex and Harold Hardrada, King of Norway, who was next in line to the Danish throne.

Christianity

9th century Celtic cross

Christianity was introduced into England by the Romans in the 3rd century. After the arrival of the *pagan** Anglo-Saxons it almost died out in England. However, some Christian Britons fled to Ireland and Wales where the Church developed separately from Rome and became known as the Celtic Church.

In 597 the Pope, the leader of the Church in Rome, sent a monk called Augustine to convert the Anglo-Saxons to Christianity. This caused conflict with the Celtic Church, which was also trying to extend its influence into England. In 664 a synod (or meeting) was held at Whitby to decide whether England should follow Celtic or Roman religious law. The synod decided in favour of Rome. By the 8th century England was a Christian country under the influence of the Roman Church.

† *'Unready' was used to mean badly advised.*

The Normans

The Normans, or 'northmen', were descended from Vikings who had settled in northern France during the 9th century. In 911 they accepted the French king as their *overlord**, and converted to *Christianity** in return for control over the area now known as Normandy.

In 1066 King Edward the Confessor of England died and was succeeded by Harold, Earl of Wessex. However, there were two other claimants to the throne: William, Duke of Normandy and Harold Hardrada of Norway. In October, Harold Hardrada invaded the north of England but was defeated at the Battle of Stamford Bridge.

The Norman invasion

The Norman invasion of England is recorded in the Bayeux Tapestry, begun in 1080.

Three days later William invaded in the south with the best cavalry in Europe. Although the Saxons were excellent foot soldiers they had never developed a large cavalry. They were used to fighting the Vikings who also fought on foot. This gave the Normans an advantage. They defeated the weary Saxons at the Battle of Hastings and William became king. It was one of the most decisive battles in English history. All subsequent kings and queens of England have been related to William in some way.

Many Saxon nobles refused to accept William as king and rebelled. Uprisings continued until the winter of 1069-70 when William subdued rebellious *shires** in the north. He made raids on Scotland too, but failed to make the Scottish king accept him as his overlord. By 1100 the Normans also controlled most of Wales, despite uprisings by the Welsh princes in 1094 and 1097.

Royal government

Once William was in control he organized a strong central government in which Normans held most positions of power. On three occasions each year he called a King's Council at which he discussed his policies with all the chief nobles and church leaders.

At other times the king ruled the country through the officials in his household, who had political as well as domestic duties. Many government departments today developed from the jobs of these Norman officers. For example, the Exchequer (the financial department) is named after the chequered cloth which was used to help count taxes.

William retained the Anglo-Saxon sheriffs as his representatives in the shires. They kept law and order and collected taxes.

Castles

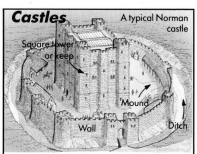

A typical Norman castle

Square tower or keep

Mound

Wall

Ditch

Before the Norman invasion there were very few castles in Britain, although they had existed in France since the 9th century. Castles were important as strongholds from which the local lord could control the countryside. They were also an effective way of protecting expensive war-horses.

Early castles consisted of an earth mound with wooden buildings surrounded by a wall and a ditch. These were called *motte* (mound) and *bailey* (courtyard) castles. The wooden buildings were later rebuilt in stone. The White Tower at the Tower of London, built in 1078, is one of the earliest examples.

The feudal system

The Normans introduced a new social system into England which is known as feudalism. It was based on a complex chain of duties, rights and loyalties, and governed such aspects of life as land ownership, army service and taxes.

Everyone owed total loyalty to the king.

The king

The king granted *fiefs* (large areas of land) to his chief nobles.

Noble

The nobles, or 'tenants-in-chief', granted smaller areas called manors to lesser nobles and knights.

Knight

The knights distributed land to the peasants and maintained law and order.

Peasant

The nobles paid *dues** to the king and fought with their knights in his army for 40 days a year.

The knights paid dues to their lord and had to fight with him in the king's army.

There were two types of peasant. Free peasants owned or rented land; *villeins* paid their lord dues and worked on his land as well as their own.

The Domesday Book

William I commissioned the *Domesday Survey* in 1086. It recorded the details of all land holdings in the country. This enabled William to see how rich each area was so he could demand taxes accordingly.

Relations with France

Throughout William's reign, there were plots and rebellions against him in France. These were supported by the King of France and the Count of Anjou, both of whom felt threatened by his power and wealth.

When William died in 1089, he left Normandy to his eldest son Robert and England to his second son William II, who was succeeded in 1100 by a third brother, Henry I. The split inheritance caused many problems because each son coveted the land and power of the other.

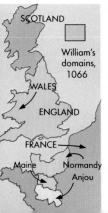

SCOTLAND

William's domains, 1066

WALES

ENGLAND

FRANCE

Maine   Normandy

Anjou

Nobles who held land on both sides of the English Channel found it difficult to serve two hostile overlords at once. After two attempts by William II, Henry I successfully invaded and *annexed** Normandy in 1106. Robert died in prison in 1134.

The civil war

Henry's only legitimate son, William, drowned in 1120, and the line of succession came under threat. In 1128 Henry married his daughter Matilda to Geoffrey of Anjou, (to end the rivalry with Anjou), and made the nobles promise to recognize her as his heir.

However, when Henry died in 1135, the barons accepted his nephew Stephen of Blois as king. In 1139 Matilda claimed the throne. Civil war followed, but in 1153 a compromise was finally reached. Stephen continued to rule, but Matilda's son, Henry of Anjou, became his heir.

Key dates

1066	The Battle of Hastings
1066-89	Reign of William I
1086	The Domesday Survey
1089-1100	Reign of William II
1100-35	Reign of Henry I
1106	Henry I annexes Normandy.
1135-54	Reign of Stephen
1139-53	Civil war
1154-89	Reign of Henry II

The Plantagenets

Henry II (1154-89) was the first of the Plantagenet kings. The name comes from *planta genista* (Latin for broom plant), the emblem of Henry's father, Geoffrey of Anjou. Henry fought in France and Wales (see page 15) and changed the legal system so all trials had to be heard in proper courts instead of allowing *trial by combat**. He wanted priests to be tried in civil courts, not Church courts (see page 13), but was opposed by Thomas à Becket, the Archbishop of Canterbury†. In 1170 Becket was killed by four of Henry's knights. Henry was horrified. To pacify the Pope he decided to leave the Church courts as they were.

The tomb of Eleanor of Aquitaine, wife of Henry II.

Richard I and King John

Richard I (1189-99), known as 'the Lionheart', spent most of his reign on *crusade** and at war in France. His brother John (1199-1216) made enemies among the *barons** and the clergy.

Richard I

He imposed heavy taxes which led to civil unrest. In 1215 the barons made him sign the *Magna Carta*, a document establishing their right to be consulted on such matters as taxation.

In 1205 he clashed with the Pope over the choice of a new archbishop. The Pope *excommunicated** him in 1208, and laid an *interdict** on England and Wales which was not lifted until 1213.

Henry III and civil war

John's son, Henry III (1216-72), angered the barons by giving financial and political aid to many of his foreign friends and relatives. In 1258 they forced him to consult a council of barons before making decisions. Conflict led to civil war (1264-65). Henry was captured but was later restored to the throne.

Parliament

In 1264 the barons' leader, Simon de Montfort, called a meeting, known as a parliament. A number of knights and representatives of certain towns were invited to attend. From 1295 each town and *shire** sent two spokesmen. These were the first members of Parliament.

Manuscript showing Edward I at a meeting of Parliament.

The word Parliament comes from the French word *parler*, which means 'to speak'.

Kings gradually began to consult Parliament before raising taxes to pay for specific things like war. Soon Parliament insisted on being consulted on all taxes. In 1332 it first met in two buildings (or 'Houses'). The nobility and the clergy met in the House of Lords, and town and shire spokesmen met in the House of Commons. By 1600 all laws had to be approved by both Houses.

Edward I and Edward II

Henry III's son Edward I (1272-1307) made many legal reforms and was called 'the Law Giver'. He tried to unite England and Scotland by claiming the Scottish throne (see page 14).

Edward II (1307-27) was weak and easily influenced. The barons did not trust him and in 1311 they banded together to limit his powers. Later Edward gradually regained control despite his defeat in Scotland (see page 14). However, he was deposed in 1327 by his wife, Isabelle of France, and her lover Roger Mortimer. He died the same year, probably murdered.

Edward III

Edward's son, Edward III (1327-77), took control from his mother Isabelle in 1330. In spite of constant war (see pages 14-15), Edward restored royal prestige, regained the support of his barons and improved trade. However, the economy deteriorated because of war and the Black Death (see page 16).

Edward III's son, Edward, was known as the 'Black Prince' because of his black armour. He died in battle in 1376.

Richard II

Richard II (1377-99) was Edward's young grandson. His uncle John of Gaunt, Duke of Lancaster, was *regent** until Richard took control in 1385. Richard was considered obstinate and irresponsible both by his barons and by Parliament. In 1386 the barons rebelled, but Richard regained control and gradually banished or executed his critics. Gaunt's son Henry Bolingbroke was exiled. Gaunt died in 1399 and Richard confiscated his estates. Henry returned to claim them, forced Richard to *abdicate**, and became king himself. Richard died in 1400. He is thought to have been murdered.

Henry IV and Henry V

Henry IV's reign (1399-1413) was turbulent, and there were several rebellions in support of other claimants to the throne. In 1403 the nobles of Wales and Northumberland rebelled, but Henry defeated them at the Battle of Shrewsbury (1403). He died in 1413. His son Henry V (1413-22) spent most of his reign at war in France where he extended English territory (see page 14).

Henry V

The Wars of the Roses

The Wars of the Roses is the name given to the struggle for power between the two factions of the royal family – the houses of York and Lancaster. They are named after the emblems of the two rivals.

The white rose of York

The red rose of Lancaster

Bitter rivalries developed during the *minority** reign of the Lancastrian Henry VI (1422-71). He could not control his nobles and lost most of the land that Henry V had gained in France. Fighting broke out in 1455. Richard of York led the Yorkists but was killed in 1460. In 1461 his son Edward defeated Henry and was crowned Edward IV (1461-83), although Henry was briefly reinstated between 1469 and 1471.

Edward ruled well, enforcing law and order, improving trade and making alliances with Brittany, Burgundy and Scotland. When he died, doubt was cast on the legitimacy of his young heir, Edward, who was never crowned. The boy's uncle Richard of Gloucester took the throne as Richard III (1483-85). Edward and his brother (known as the Princes in the Tower) disappeared, presumed murdered. In 1485 Henry Tudor, a Lancastrian, defeated Richard at the Battle of Bosworth and became Henry VII (see page 18).

Battles of the Wars of the Roses

1455   Yorkist victory at St. Albans

1460   Yorkist victory at Northampton
Lancastrian victory at Wakefield

1461   Edward of York, supported by the Earl of Warwick, defeats Henry VI at Mortimer's Cross and becomes Edward IV.

1469   Warwick changes sides and defeats Edward at Edgecote. Henry VI regains the throne.

1471   Edward IV defeats Warwick at Barnet and regains the throne. Henry VI is murdered.

1485   Battle of Bosworth – Henry Tudor defeats Richard III and becomes Henry VII.

The Church in the Middle Ages

In the Middle Ages, religion played a very important part in daily life. Most western Europeans belonged to the Roman Catholic Church, which was based in Rome. The Pope, leader of the Roman Catholic Church, dictated doctrine and organization, appointed Church officials, and claimed spiritual power over all political leaders. This often led to tension between Church and State. This diagram shows how the Church was organized in Britain.

Church organization in England

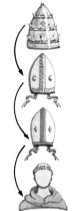

The Pope ruled the Church from Rome and all churchmen owed him loyalty.

Two archbishops led the Church in England.

Bishops were in charge of large areas called *dioceses*.

Dioceses were divided into smaller areas called parishes, which were run by priests.

The king gave *fiefs** to bishops and abbots (heads of monasteries) and in return they owed him *dues**. Although the Pope had authority over the king in religious affairs they sometimes disagreed on other matters. This meant churchmen sometimes had divided loyalties.

Monasteries

Monks and nuns were men and women who made religious *vows** and dedicated their lives to God. They lived in communities called monasteries (for the monks) and convents (for the nuns). In addition to working and praying, they looked after the poor and sick and sheltered travellers. These communities played an important part in society. By 1170 there were 900 of them in England.

Monasteries often had schools attached to them for the education of future priests and monks but boys from noble families could also attend. Boys were taught Latin, the language of the Church, as well as other subjects.

The monks wrote out religious texts and decorated them with gold and brilliant colours. These are known as illuminated manuscripts.

Education

Late in the 12th century, several universities were founded in Europe. Britain's oldest universities are Oxford (c.1214). Although schools were usually attached to monasteries, from the 14th century, many schools were founded independently by rich patrons.

Pilgrimages

Many people went on religious journeys called pilgrimages in order to pray for *miracles** or make amends for their sins. They went to places they believed were holy, such as the sites of important religious events, or churches which contained the relics of saints. Canterbury Cathedral, where St. Thomas à Becket was killed (see page 10), was a popular destination for pilgrims.

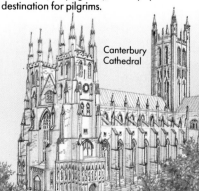

Canterbury Cathedral

The Crusades

The Crusades, or holy wars, were a series of military campaigns fought by European *Christians** to recover Palestine from the *Muslim** Turks. The capture of Jerusalem by the Turks in 1071 had led Pope Urban II to call for a crusade against them in 1095. Men from all over Europe went to fight, hoping to gain spiritual and material rewards. New orders of soldier-monks were set up to fight the Turks. These included the Knights of St John, founded in 1098.

As a result of the First Crusade, Jerusalem was captured and a new Christian kingdom was established. Later the Muslims re-organized and began driving the Christians out. They took Jerusalem in 1187. Acre, the last Christian stronghold in Palestine, was captured in 1291.

This shows the Siege of Antioch in 1098.

Relations between Church and State

In the Middle Ages there was frequent conflict between the Church and the State. Many monarchs resented the Pope's authority over them, which often interfered with matters of state.

In 1351 the English Parliament passed the Statute of Provisions, which entitled the king to make Church appointments instead of the Pope. Two years later the Statute of Praemunire was passed. This stated that clergymen suspected of crimes had to be tried in civil courts, instead of the more lenient Church courts which had existed since 1072.

Problems in the Church

From the 14th century there was increasing criticism of the clergy. Many monks and priests were badly educated, and neglected both their duties and their vows . There were also abuses of Church law such as simony (selling of Church positions), nepotism (giving positions of power to relations) and pluralism (holding several positions at once).

Criticism of the clergy sometimes even included criticism of some of the Church's teachings. This was condemned by the Church as *heresy**. Heretics who refused to change their beliefs, and witches (people thought to worship the devil) were burned alive.

John Wyclif

John Wyclif (1329-84) questioned the authority of the Pope and some important articles of faith. He also believed that everyone should be allowed to read the Bible, and so he translated it from Latin into English. His ideas were condemned as heretical and after his death his followers, known as Lollards (meaning 'babblers'), had to preach his ideas in secret.

Key dates

1054 The Great Schism — the Church divides into the Eastern Orthodox Church, based in Constantinople, and the Roman Catholic Church, based in Rome.

1072 Church courts are set up in England.

1075-1122 The Investiture Controversy — the disagreement over the control of Church appointments focuses on investiture, a ceremony in which the king gives a new bishop the symbols of his office.

1096-1099 First Crusade

1107 Henry I compromises. He stops the symbolic ceremony of investiture, but the bishops still owe him feudal duties.

1147-1149 Second Crusade

1189-1192 Third Crusade, led by Richard I.

1351 Statute of Provisions

1353 Statute of Praemunire

Plantagenet foreign affairs

Since 1066 English kings had been involved in quarrels and wars over land they held in France. England also tried to increase its control over Scotland, Wales and Ireland which led to conflict and rebellion.

The fleur-de-lis, the royal emblem of France, was on the English coat of arms until 1801.

The 100 Years' War

The 100 Years' War was in fact a series of wars between England and France which lasted from 1337 to 1453. In 1328 Charles IV of France died without a male heir. The English king, Edward III, whose mother was Isabelle of France, laid claim to the throne and war broke out in 1337.

The English won major victories at Crécy (1346), Calais (1347) and Poitiers (1356). By the Treaty of Brétigny (1360) England was left in control of south-west France. However, war began again in 1369, and during Richard II's reign France regained a lot of land.

The British won many battles because they used longbows, which shot arrows further than the bows of the French.

Hostilities were renewed in 1415 when Henry V revived England's claims. He invaded France and won important battles at Harfleur and Agincourt. France surrendered and Henry restored English control in northern France. By the Treaty of Troyes (1420) he married the French king's daughter and was made heir to the throne, in place of Charles, the king's eldest son.

Charles refused to accept this and he declared war after Henry's death in 1422. In 1429 his armies were led to victory by a peasant woman named Joan of Arc who claimed she heard voices from God. Charles was crowned king the same year, but Joan was burnt as a witch by the English in 1431. The French went on to take Paris (1436), Normandy (1449) and Guienne (1451). The war ended in 1453 and England lost all its French land except Calais.

Scotland

From the 9th century Scotland was ruled by the MacAlpin family. The Normans never conquered Scotland although border raids by both sides were common throughout the Middle Ages. In the 12th century David I (1124-53) encouraged good relations with England and granted land in southern Scotland to English *barons**. However, he was always ready to increase Scotland's power and during the civil war in England (see page 10) he took control of English land near the Scottish border – Cumberland, Westmorland, and Northumberland. England regained them in 1157.

In 1173 the Scottish king, William 'the Lion', invaded England to assist a rebellion against Henry II. He was captured and forced to accept Henry II as his *overlord**. Although later kings enforced their overlordship, Henry's son Richard I was willing to ignore his right to exert authority in Scotland in return for money to go on *crusade**.

In 1290 the main line of the MacAlpin family died out and there were 13 claimants to the throne. As overlord, Edward I was asked to choose between them. He chose a man called John Balliol (1292-96) but *deposed** him in 1296 and took the throne himself.

The Scots rebelled in 1297-98, led by a knight called William Wallace. He was executed in 1305 and there was another rebellion, led by Robert Bruce, a relative of Balliol. The English were forced out of Scotland. Bruce became king in 1306, but conflict continued and in 1314 Edward II was defeated at the Battle of Bannockburn. England finally recognised Scottish independence in 1328.

In 1371 the Scottish throne passed to the House of Stewart (later spelled Stuart – see page 22) which descended from Robert Bruce's daughter, Marjorie.

Wales

Beaumaris • Conwy • Caernarfon
Harlech • Criccieth
Aberystwyth
Builth

Welsh Marches

• Castles built by Edward I

From Anglo-Saxon times Wales was made up of small warring kingdoms. The Welsh also frequently fought the English, who sought more power and territory in Wales. English land on the Welsh border, known as the Welsh Marches, was constantly being extended. By 1100 most of south Wales was under English control. Henry II invaded the north twice but was finally defeated in 1165 by Owain, Prince of Gwynedd (1137-70).

Owain's grandson Llwelyn the Great (1194-1240) was accepted as overlord by most of the Welsh princes. He repelled English invasions in 1211 and 1213. His grandson Llwelyn ap Grufydd (1246-82) extended his control even further and became sole Welsh ruler in 1254. He was recognized by Henry III as Prince of Wales in 1267, and in return he accepted Henry as his overlord.

However, in 1277 Edward I of England invaded Wales after Llwelyn refused to swear loyalty to him. By the Statute of Wales (1284), the country became part of the English *royal domain** and was reorganized into five counties.

A reconstruction of Harlech Castle

Strong towers and gatehouses   Defensive wall

Edward built strong castles, based on new European models, and introduced English criminal law. In an attempt to gain the loyalty of the Welsh, he made his Welsh-born son Prince of Wales in 1301. The eldest son of the English monarch has held this title ever since.

Ireland

From Roman times Ireland consisted of warring kingdoms. The Vikings (see page 7) began raiding the country in 795 and some of them settled there, founding the first Irish towns. In 831 Thorgist, a Viking chief, declared himself High King of all Ireland (ruler over all the other kings). The native Irish fought their Viking rulers for many years. Eventually in 1002 an Irish leader, Brian Boru of Munster, seized control and became High King. He defeated the Vikings at the Battle of Clontarf in 1014.

In 1166 the High King, Rory O'Connor, banished the King of Leinster, who then asked Henry II for military aid. In 1170 Henry sent an army led by Richard de Clare (known as 'Strongbow') and Leinster's lands were restored. Henry landed in Ireland in 1171 and was accepted by the Irish kings as their overlord.

English territory

Irish territory

Dublin •
Limerick • The Pale
Waterford
Cork

The extent of English control in Ireland in 1307

During the 13th century, many Anglo-Norman barons settled in Ireland. They introduced feudalism (see page 9) and forced the native Irish to become *serfs**.

During this time a parliament evolved, made up of Anglo-Irish nobles who did not wish to associate with the native Irish. In 1366 marriage between the Irish and the English was banned, and Irish laws and customs were forbidden in English areas.

By 1400 only the west of Ireland was under the control of Irish kings. The rest was ruled by barons, apart from Dublin, which was part of the English royal domain. Dublin was surrounded by a fortified enclosure, known as the Pale.

The medieval economy

Society in the Middle Ages was based on the feudal system (see page 9) and most people lived and worked on the land. In 1086 this applied to over 90% of the population. Farming was based around a noble's estate, called a manor, which was divided between him and the peasants who lived on it. *Villeins** worked part-time on the lord's land and paid *dues** in return for land of their own. Free peasants owned land or rented it from the lord of the manor.

A typical medieval manor

Manor house

Church

Moat

Wheat

Cottage gardens

Pasture

The fields were divided into strips.

Fallow

The Norman kings set aside large areas of forest (such as Sherwood Forest) for hunting.

The three field system

In each manor the peasants' land was split into three large fields, which in turn were divided into strips. Each peasant farmed several strips scattered over each field. This meant it was easier for the peasants to farm the fields jointly. Each year two fields were planted with crops while the third remained fallow (unused). This scheme was rotated so that one field lay fallow every three years, to allow the soil to recover its richness. Each peasant could graze animals on the common and had a cottage garden for growing vegetables.

The population grows

Between the 11th and 14th centuries, England's population doubled. Marshes and woods (including some royal forest) were cleared to grow more crops. In the 12th century many landlords introduced a system called commutation. This enabled villeins to avoid working on the noble's land if they paid a fee. Landlords then paid landless men low wages to work for them, and so made a profit.

Famine and plague

By the 14th century, the population had increased so much that there was a food shortage. As a result food prices rose and many people died from starvation. In 1348 a plague known as the Black Death swept across Europe, and in Britain one third of the population died in 18 months. Suddenly there were not enough people to work the land. Labourers were able to demand higher wages and farmers paid lower rents.

The Peasants' Revolt

The landlords attempted to reverse this situation and in 1351 a law was passed to keep wages down. This caused great resentment. In 1381 peasants in Kent, Essex and East Anglia rebelled when a high *poll tax** was set. Peasants from Kent and Essex marched to London to protest. Richard II pardoned them and promised to meet their demands. But the peasants were attacked by the soldiers of the Lord Mayor of London. Their leader Wat Tyler was murdered and the promises were broken.

The decline of feudalism

the manorial system eventually broke down and villeinage died out. Wages rose and rents were reduced. Nobles could no longer afford to farm such large manors, so they rented out blocks of land to individual peasant farmers. In this way the number of land-owning peasants increased.

Towns and trade

Towns began as centres where people came to trade, and so they were usually situated at good trading sites, such as at a major crossroads or by a river. As the population of England increased, more towns grew up. Between 1100 and 1300, about 140 new towns appeared. Although townspeople were 'freemen' they were under the jurisdiction of the local lord. However, if the king or the local lord agreed, the people could pay for a document called a *charter**, which allowed them to govern their town themselves and set their own taxes.

Some towns were allowed to hold big annual fairs which were also attended by foreign traders.

Guilds

The first guilds, associations of merchants and craftsmen, were established in the 11th century. By the 12th century each trade had its own guild. Guilds set wages and prices, and established standards of work and trading practice. Boys were apprenticed (taught by a master craftsman) for up to seven years before they became qualified craftsmen.

The cloth industry

In the Middle Ages wool was England's most important export. It was usually sold to foreign traders who had it made into cloth in Flanders† or Italy. British cloth was of poor quality until the 12th century, when a machine called a fulling mill was introduced. This improved the quality of the finished cloth. As a result, more wool was made into cloth before it was sold. Fulling mills relied on running water for power, so the cloth industry moved away from towns into country areas where both sheep and water could be found. Rural cloth-workers were poorly paid as they were not protected by guilds. By the 15th century the whole industry was run by rich merchants.

Imports and exports

England imported timber, pitch, tar and furs from the Baltic; wines, metal goods and leather from France; and spices, sugar, silks and jewels from the East. Its main exports were wool, cloth, tin, lead and grain. At first foreign traders bought English goods and sold them abroad but in the 14th century English merchants began to take over and foreigners were charged high duties to take goods out of the country. In 1407 a group of English merchants who called themselves the Merchant Adventurers formed an association to trade overseas. By 1550 they controlled about 75% of England's foreign trade. Ship design was improved, making long sea journeys easier.

Knights and chivalry

Knights (see page 9) were trained warriors from noble families who fought on horseback. They were supposed to follow a rigid code of conduct, fighting only for just causes and protecting the weak.

Before becoming a knight, a boy was trained as a page (attendant) in another knight's castle. When he was about 15 he became a squire (knight's assistant), following the lord into battle.

Knights wore personal symbols so that they could be recognized in battle. In the 12th century, these evolved into coats of arms.

In times of peace, knights fought in mock battles or in single combat at tournaments called *jousts*

The early Tudors

Henry Tudor   Elizabeth of York

Henry Tudor, heir to the Lancastrian line (see page 11), became Henry VII (1485-1509), the first of the Tudor kings. To secure his hold on the throne and ensure the succession, he married Edward IV's daughter Elizabeth of York. He also imprisoned, banished or executed other possible rivals and put down two rebellions. The first, in 1487, tried to put a boy called Lambert Simnel on the throne, claiming he was Edward IV's nephew, the Earl of Warwick. The second, in 1497, was led by Perkin Warbeck, who claimed to be Edward IV's youngest son, Richard Duke of York.

Henry involved himself in the day-to-day details of government. Although he had a council of nobles and churchmen, he increasingly relied on advisers from the merchant and professional classes. Henry radically improved royal revenues by promoting trade and imposing new taxes.

Henry avoided foreign wars. He made peace treaties with Spain (1489), France (1492) and Scotland (1497). He married his eldest son Arthur to Catherine of Aragon, a Spanish princess, and his daughter Margaret to James IV of Scotland. When Arthur died Catherine married his brother Henry (later Henry VIII).

Henry VIII (1509-47)

Henry VIII

Henry VIII had six wives: Catherine of Aragon, Anne Boleyn, Jane Seymour, Anne of Cleves, Catherine Howard and Catherine Parr. His reign was marked by foreign wars and by religious upheaval.

Government

Henry's council, like his father's, included members from the professional classes. In the 1530s Henry cut his council to 20 members and it became known as the Privy Council. Henry's most famous ministers were Cardinal Wolsey (1515-29), Sir Thomas More (1529-35) and Thomas Cromwell (1535-40).

Foreign affairs

The cost of war rose in the 16th century with the increasing use of guns. Although Henry's advisers discouraged him from going to war, he wanted to regain English lands in France (see page 14). He declared war in 1511 but made peace the next year. Louis XII of France died in 1515 and relations with the new king, Francis I, were more strained. Wolsey organized a peace treaty in 1518. Although Henry and Francis met in 1520 to discuss terms, England and France were at war again from 1520 to 1525.

The place where Henry and Francis met became known as the Field of the Cloth of Gold.

Henry invaded France again in 1543, making peace in 1546. England gained little from the war, and when Henry died the government was virtually bankrupt.

The succession

Henry needed a son to secure the succession, but only his daughter Mary had survived infancy. He wanted to divorce Catherine and marry Anne Boleyn. Royal marriages could sometimes be ended for political reasons, but only with the Pope's consent. However, Pope Clement VII was being held prisoner by Catherine's nephew, Charles V of Spain. As the Pope did not wish to anger Charles, he refused to grant the divorce.

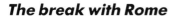

The break with Rome

To get what he wanted Henry decided to take control of the Church in England. He married Anne in 1533 and their daughter Elizabeth was born later that year. In 1534 Parliament passed the Act of Supremacy which declared Henry the Supreme Head of the English Church. Anne's children became first in line to the throne. People were made to take an oath accepting Henry's heirs, and his position as Head of the Church in England. Sir Thomas More, John Fisher, Bishop of Rochester, and several others who refused to take the oath, were executed for *treason**. In 1535 the Pope *excommunicated** Henry for *heresy**.

Meanwhile in mainland Europe reformers known as Protestants were rejecting many of the teachings of the Roman Catholic Church. However, although Henry denied the Pope's authority, he did not accept Protestant doctrines. In 1536 he issued the 6 Articles, which set out points of Catholic doctrine still to be followed.

Between 1536 and 1539 Henry closed all the convents and monasteries in England on the pretext that they were corrupt or not economically viable. Most of them were sold and many were destroyed. This is known as the dissolution of the monasteries.

The ruins of Fountains Abbey in Yorkshire

Edward VI (1547-53) and Lady Jane Grey

Edward VI, Henry's son by Jane Seymour, became king when he was nine years old. His uncle the Duke of Somerset acted as *regent**. Somerset introduced radical changes in religion which brought the Church closer to European Protestantism.

In 1551 the Duke of Northumberland took power as regent. He persuaded Edward to disinherit his sisters, Mary and Elizabeth, and to name as his heir, his cousin Lady Jane Grey. She was married to Northumberland's son, Guildford Dudley. When Edward died in 1553, Jane ruled for nine days before Mary Tudor seized power. Jane, Dudley and Northumberland were all executed.

Edward VI

Relations with Scotland

England and Scotland were often on bad terms during Henry VIII's reign, and in 1512 James IV of Scotland invaded England. Henry was in France, but his wife, Catherine, sent troops. The Scots were defeated at the Battle of Flodden (1513) and James was killed. His young son, James V, became king, and the country was ruled by regents until 1528. In 1538 James married Mary of Guise, a French Catholic princess. This drew him into an alliance with France which led to war with England in 1542. The Scots were defeated at Solway Moss and James V died soon afterwards. His baby, Mary, became queen (1542-67).

English troops were sent to Scotland in 1546 and unsuccessfully tried to force a marriage alliance between Mary and Henry's son, Edward. The Scots were defeated at the Battle of Pinkie, and in 1547 Mary was sent to France by her French mother. She married Francis, heir to the French throne, but returned to Scotland after his death in 1560.

Key dates

1487 and **1497**   Rebellions in support of pretenders to the throne

1534   Act of Supremacy

1536   Wales is united with England. It is split into *shires** and given the same laws and rights as England.

1536-39   Dissolution of the monasteries

1549   Act of Uniformity – the First English Prayer Book (modified in 1552) becomes the only permitted prayer book.

19

The later Tudors

Mary Tudor (1553-58) immediately reinstated Catholicism and repealed all Protestant legislation. During her reign over 300 Protestants who refused to accept Catholicism were burnt as *heretics**. Many others fled to mainland Europe.

Mary wanted a child to ensure the Catholic succession. Despite public and parliamentary oposition, she married Philip II of Spain in 1554. She died childless in 1558, and was succeeded by her 25-year-old half-sister Elizabeth.

Elizabeth I (1558-1603)

Elizabeth I pursued successful policies at home and abroad. The arts flourished under her patronage and her reign is considered to be the high point of the English Renaissance (see below). Nevertheless there were tensions: the economy was weak, there were deep-seated religious divisions and England's relations with Scotland, France and Spain were strained.

Elizabeth I

Government

Elizabeth inherited a weak economy. Henry VIII, Mary and Edward VI had all debased the coinage by reducing the amount of silver or gold in each coin, so more money could be minted. This led to rising prices and unemployment.

Elizabeth took steps to improve the situation. Between 1560 and 1561, she recalled all the debased coins and issued new ones. She rarely imposed new taxes to raise money. Instead, she sold royal lands and *charters**, raised loans and gained revenue from exploration abroad.

In an attempt to deal with social problems caused by unemployment, Poor Laws were passed in 1553, 1597 and 1601. Each parish became responsible for looking after its own poor.

Religion

Elizabeth was Protestant, but she wanted the Church to be organized so that it would be acceptable to most of her subjects. She reinstated Henry VIII's legislation, and became Supreme Governor of the English (or Anglican) Church. In 1563 its doctrines were defined in the 39 Articles. These offended Catholics, and also some radical Protestants, known as Puritans, who wanted greater changes to be made.

In 1570 the Pope *excommunicated** Elizabeth and declared it the duty of all Catholics to try to *depose** her. In England suspicion of Catholics became widespread. Many Jesuit priests, sent from Rome to undermine the Anglican Church and convert England back to Catholicism, were caught and executed.

Elizabeth's Catholic cousin, Mary Queen of Scots (see page 19), laid claim to the English throne in 1559 and became a focus for Catholic rebellion. From 1569 she was involved in four plots against Elizabeth. She was finally charged with *treason** and executed in 1587.

The English Renaissance

The arts flourished in England during Elizabeth's reign with the work of such people as the writers William Shakespeare (1564-1616) and Christopher Marlowe (1564-93), the painter Nicholas Hilliard (1547-1619), and the composer William Byrd (1543-1623). This period is sometimes known as the English Renaissance.

Portrait miniatures by Nicholas Hilliard were very popular.

Many of Shakespeare's plays were performed at the Swan Theatre in London.

Foreign policy

Elizabeth defended herself from the dangers posed by European Catholic monarchs by supporting Protestant groups involved in civil wars in France (1562-1598), Scotland (1559-67) and the Spanish Netherlands (1568-1648).

By the 1570s relations with Spain had deteriorated. The Spaniards were enraged by English attacks on Spanish ships in the New World (see opposite) and supported revolts in Ireland against English rule. Philip II of Spain built a vast fleet of ships, called the Armada, to invade England. It set sail in 1588, but the English set many of the ships on fire off the coast of France, and the rest were destroyed by storms.

In the last years of Elizabeth's reign England was constantly at war with Spain – both at sea and in the Netherlands. In France, Elizabeth helped to establish Henry of Navarre, a Protestant prince, on the French throne.

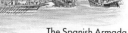

The Spanish Armada

Ireland under the Tudors

During Elizabeth's reign Irish resentment of English rule came to a head. In 1494 an English act of Parliament had stated that Ireland's Parliament (see page 11) could only be called with the consent of the English king. Topics for discussion had to be agreed by him first. Following a rebellion against the Act of Supremacy in 1534, Henry VIII decided that all acts of the English Parliament should also apply to Ireland. In 1541 he changed his title from 'Lord' to 'King' of Ireland. Ireland was in a constant state of unrest during Elizabeth's reign. Several uprisings were put down, including one ending in 1602 in which the Irish were helped by the Spaniards.

Exploration

In the 15th and 16th centuries European seafarers began to explore the world. Until then Europeans only had knowledge of the north and west coasts of Africa and overland routes to the East.

16th century navigational instruments.

Sea routes to the East were first pioneered by Portuguese and Spanish navigators. They also sailed west and discovered America which became known as the New World. Spain took control of Portugal in 1580 and refused to give the French and the English trading rights in the New World and in the East Indies. As a result, they began to attack and loot Spanish treasure ships. Many expeditions left England each year, led by men such as Francis Drake (the first Englishman to sail around the world), Walter Ralegh and John Hawkins. The profits from these expeditions were considerable.

The succession

Elizabeth never married, although Parliament continually urged her to do so. In 1587 she accepted James VI of Scotland, the Protestant son of Mary Queen of Scots (see page 19), as her heir. Elizabeth died in 1603 and James became James I of England.

Key dates

1553-58 Reign of Mary

1559-1603 Reign of Elizabeth 1

1559 Treaty of Câteau Cambrésis – England loses Calais, its last piece of French territory.

1559-67 Civil war in Scotland between the Presbyterians (Scottish Protestants), led by John Knox, and the Catholics. Presbyterianism becomes Scotland's established religion.

1588 The Spanish Armada is defeated.

The early Stuarts

During the reigns of the first two Stuart[†] kings, James I (1603-25) and his son, Charles I (1625-49), there was growing hostility between the

James I

king and Parliament, which finally ended in civil war. Parliament was becoming increasingly dominated by groups of extreme Protestants known as Puritans. They wanted to outlaw Catholicism and radically reform the Anglican Church, and some even wanted to abolish it.

The king controlled religious and foreign policy and appointed his own advisers. Parliament was meant to act in an advisory capacity, to introduce and to approve new laws and taxes and grant extra funds for emergencies, such as war. In return the king paid the costs of government from his own income, which mainly derived from crown lands and feudal dues (see page 9). However, from Elizabethan times, this income was inadequate to cover all the costs of government. This led to problems, as Parliament was reluctant to grant extra funds without receiving more influence over foreign and religious policy.

James and Charles both tried to resist Parliament's attempts to increase its own authority, by ruling without Parliament for years at a time. They believed they were chosen by God and responsible only to God for their actions. This theory is known as the Divine Right of Kings.

James I (1603-25)

James ended an expensive war with Catholic Spain in 1604, to the disapproval of the Puritans.

*Inflation** increased the costs of government and in 1604 James asked Parliament to grant extra funds. Parliament refused so instead James increased *customs and excise duties** without receiving their approval. He also began to sell more trading *monopolies**, which caused resentment in Parliament.

Charles I (1625-49)

The Commons distrusted Charles I, suspecting him of Catholic sympathies. He married a French Catholic princess, Henrietta Maria, and appointed William Laud (whom the Puritans considered to be too Catholic in his views) as Archbishop of Canterbury in 1633.

England was at war with France from 1626 to 1630 and supported the Huguenots (French Protestants). Charles called Parliaments in 1626 and 1628 but dissolved them both after they refused to grant money without first discussing religious and political matters. They also tried to *impeach** his friend the Duke of Buckingham. In a third Parliament in 1629, the Commons produced resolutions against customs and excise duties and Catholicism. The same year he began to reintroduce old taxes to gain more revenue. He also issued a proclamation which implied that he did not intend calling Parliament again during his reign.

In 1630 England withdrew from war with both France and Spain, due to lack of funds. Charles did not call Parliament again until 1640. This period is sometimes called the 11 years' Tyranny. During this time he built up his navy to rival that of the Dutch, who had become Europe's leading maritime nation. To cover the cost, he levied an old tax called Ship Money on both coastal and inland areas.

Early American colonies

The first successful *colony** was set up in Virginia in 1607. Some Puritans and Catholics who disliked England's religious laws emigrated to America. In 1620 a group of Puritans, known as the Pilgrim Fathers, set sail in the Mayflower. They settled in an area they called New England. A Catholic colony was set up in Maryland in 1632.

Puritans

†Stuart was originally spelled 'Stewart' (see page 14).

War with Scotland

Most people in Scotland were *Presbyterian** and riots broke out when Charles attempted to introduce Anglicanism there. Some Scots signed a document called the National Covenant, declaring their refusal to accept any doctrinal changes not approved by the Presbyterian Church. They became known as Covenanters.

Charles retaliated by declaring war on the Scots in 1639. In 1640 he called Parliament to raise money but it again took the opportunity to insist on its right to be involved in religious and foreign policy. Charles dissolved it after three weeks, but the Scots invaded the north of England and Parliament was recalled. It became known as the Long Parliament as it was not officially dissolved until 1660. To get his way Charles agreed to some of its demands: to call a Parliament at least every three years, to ask its consent to levy taxes and to make peace with the Scottish Covenanters on their terms.

The English Civil War

The Commons took advantage of its new powers and in 1641 started proceedings to abolish bishops and the English Prayer Book. They also imprisoned and eventually executed Charles' chief minister, the Earl of Strafford, and the Archbishop of Canterbury, William Laud. In 1642 the Commons presented Charles with a series of proposals (the 19 Propositions) which would have given them power over the king. Charles rejected them. As a result both sides raised armies and civil war broke out.

The Parliamentarians (known as Roundheads) had the support of London and other important ports, which helped finance their military campaigns. They set up a disciplined army, known as the New Model Army, trained by one of their leaders, Oliver Cromwell. In 1643 Parliament gained the Covenanters' support by promising to establish Presbyterianism in England, Wales and

Ireland. After many battles, the Royalists (known as Cavaliers) were finally defeated at the Battle of Naseby in 1645. In 1646 the king surrendered to the Covenanters who handed him over to Parliament.

Royalist

Roundhead   • Major battlefields

Parliament then tried to impose Presbyterianism. This was resisted by many army leaders, including Oliver Cromwell, who belonged to other Puritan groups such as the *Independents**. In 1647 Charles began negotiating with the Commons. At the same time he began secret talks with the Scots, who were disappointed by their alliance with Parliament. In 1648 the Scots declared war in support of Charles but he was captured by the Roundheads and put on trial for *treason**. Cromwell dismissed all MPs† who still sympathized with the king and would oppose his trial. The 90 remaining MPs were known as the Rump. Charles was found guilty of *treason** and executed in 1649.

Key dates: the Civil War

1641 Battle of Edgehill (the first battle of the war) ends in a *stalemate**.

1644 Battle of Marston Moor – a Parliamentary victory

1644 Battle of Lostwithiel – a Royalist victory; Battle of Tippermuir – Royalist victory; Battle of Cropredy Bridge – Royalist victory.

1645 Battle of Naseby – Parliament defeats Charles I and wins control of the country.

1648 The second civil war

1649 Charles I is tried and executed.

†*MP stands for Member of Parliament (see page 10).*

The later Stuarts

Oliver Cromwell

In 1649 a *republic*, known as the Commonwealth was set up in England. The Commons and a council of state, led by Oliver Cromwell, were to rule it.

Cromwell suppressed the Levellers (a group that emerged during the Civil War and agitated for greater *democracy*) and defeated revolts in Scotland and Ireland. There was tension between the Commons and the army, as army pay was in arrears.

In 1653 Cromwell replaced the Rump (see page 23) with 140 Puritan MPs, but dismissed them the same year and made himself ruler, under the title of Lord Protector. Unable to find a co-operative Parliament, he split England into 11 areas, each ruled by army leaders.

Cromwell recalled Parliament in 1656 but discharged it when it criticized his role as Lord Protector. He died in 1658 and his son Richard, an ineffective ruler, succeeded him. In 1659, the army deposed him and recalled Parliament who invited Charles I's son, Charles II back to England.

Ireland 1601-1714

Many English Protestants settled in *Ulster* in James I's reign. This led to conflict with the native Irish who resented English rule and their own lack of political rights. Catholic royalists rose against Cromwell in 1649 but were massacred at Wexford and Drogheda. In 1652 the English further enraged the Irish by giving two-thirds of Irish land to English Protestants.

In 1689 the exiled James II (see opposite) landed an army in Ireland. The Irish welcomed him and besieged the Protestants at Londonderry. William of Orange (see opposite) rescued them and went on to defeat James at the Battle of the Boyne (1690). The Catholics gave in and in 1692 were barred from owning land or voting. The Protestants became known as Orangemen.

Charles II (1660-85)

In 1660 Parliament restored the monarchy, but limited the king's powers and increased its own. The Anglican Church was reinstated as England's official Church. Charles II was willing to allow his subjects to follow any religion, but the new MPs were suspicious of both Catholics and Puritans. They limited their *religious freedom*, and barred them from holding army or government posts.

In 1678 a man named Titus Oates falsely accused some leading Catholics of planning to murder Charles and put his Catholic brother James on the throne. This became known as the Popish Plot. Some Catholics were executed and in 1683 it became illegal for Catholics to sit in the House of Lords.

Foreign policy

The reign of Charles II was marked by tensions with both Holland and France. England and Holland were trading and *colonial* rivals, and England was suspicious of the expansionist aims of the French king, Louis XIV. War broke out between England and Holland in 1665 after England seized New Amsterdam (a Dutch colony in North America, now New York). The fighting lasted until 1667. In 1668 they joined forces and made a treaty against France. However, Charles, who had secret Catholic sympathies, did not like supporting Holland. He was also deeply in debt. Louis XIV offered him large *subsidies* in return for his support, and in 1670 England and France became allies. England and Holland were at war again from 1672 until 1674.

Bubonic plague broke out in England in 1665, killing 68,000 people in London alone. A year later much of the city was destroyed by a fire which raged for four days.

St Paul's Church was destroyed.

Political parties

From 1668 Charles ruled with a council of five men, known as the Cabal. It broke up in 1672 and two of its members led a group of MPs against the king's policies. They became known as the Country Party. The king's supporters were called the Court Party. By 1681 both had aquired nicknames – the Country Party became known as *Whigs* and the Court party were called *Tories*.

The royal succession

As Charles had no legitimate children, his brother James was heir to the throne. Although James was Catholic the Whigs tolerated this, because his heirs, his daughters Mary and Anne, were both Protestant. However, when James married a Catholic in 1673, it posed the threat of a Catholic male heir. The Whigs tried unsuccessfully to exclude James from the succession. Some leading Whigs were

James II
Charles II

involved in a plot to kill both James and Charles. On Charles' death, one of his illegitimate sons, the Duke of Monmouth, tried to seize the throne. James defeated him at the Battle of Sedgemoor (1685).

James II 1685-89

James angered the Commons by giving Catholics important government and army posts, and by granting religious freedom. In June 1688 James had a son, thus ensuring a Catholic succession. At the request of some leading MPs, James' daughter Mary and her husband William of Orange invaded England and James fled to France. This is often known as the Glorious Revolution.

St Paul's Church was rebuilt by Christopher Wren in 1673-1711.

William III (1689-1702) and Mary II (1689-94)

In 1689 William and Mary were made joint *sovereigns*. Parliament issued the Declaration of Rights which established its power over the monarchy and excluded Catholics from the succession. William put down *Jacobite* revolts in Ireland (see opposite), and in Scotland, where most *Highland* clans remained loyal to James II. William defeated the Scottish Highlanders with the aid of the *Lowlanders*. He became unpopular in England for raising taxes to go to war with France on Holland's behalf (1689-97) and for giving government posts to foreigners.

Queen Anne 1702-14

For most of Anne's reign England was at war with Spain (see page 30). In 1707 the Scottish Parliament voted for union with England, in return for commercial concessions. The Scots kept their own legal system and *Presbyterian* Church, but their MPs now sat at Westminster.

All Anne's children died, and in 1701 her Protestant cousin Sophia of Hanover, was declared her heir. Sophia died in 1714 and her son George became next in line to the throne (see page 28).

Key dates : The Stuarts

1603 James VI of Scotland becomes James I of England.

1642-49 The English Civil War

1649 Charles I is executed

1649-60 The Commonwealth

1650-51 Scottish Royalists are defeated. Charles II flees to France.

1660 The Restoration of the Monarchy

1665 The Great Plague

1666 The Great Fire of London

1688 The Glorious Revolution

1692 The Massacre of Glencoe – many of the Jacobite Macdonald clan are killed by the Campbells, who support William III.

1707 Act of Union with Scotland

The Agricultural Revolution

Despite industrialization (see pages 34-35) Britain's economy mainly relied on agriculture until the mid-19th century. Between 1700 and 1800 the population of England and Wales rose from 5.75 million to 9.25 million. This was caused by several factors including an increase in immigrants from Ireland and Scotland, and a decline in the number of infant deaths. The growing population brought about an agricultural crisis because farmers could not produce enough food.

New farming methods

In an attempt to increase the output of their farms, farmers began to experiment with new methods of production. New systems of crop rotation and animal breeding were introduced (see opposite) and farming machinery was improved. Farmers gradually abandoned the old system of farming land in strips (see page 16) and began to hedge off their land into larger areas, called enclosures (see opposite), which could be farmed more effectively.

Enclosures

Enclosure, the reorganization and hedging in of land, began in the 17th century but did not become common until the mid-18th century. Between 1750 and 1780 over three million acres were enclosed.

When the owners of four-fifths of a manor's strips (usually two or three rich men) wanted to enclose their land, they applied to Parliament to pass an act to make the enclosure legal. Once this was done, all the land in the village, including common and waste land, was divided up. Each landowner was given a unit of land equivalent to the area in strips which he had held in the open-field system. These units then had to be enclosed, which was expensive. As a result, farmers who did not own much land often had to sell out to larger landowners. The loss of common land meant they could no longer graze their animals either. Many villagers left the country and moved to work in the new industrial towns (see page 34).

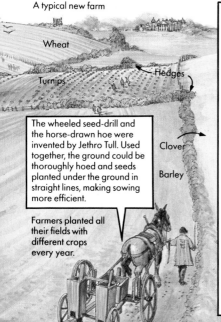

A typical new farm

Wheat

Turnips

Hedges

The wheeled seed-drill and the horse-drawn hoe were invented by Jethro Tull. Used together, the ground could be thoroughly hoed and seeds planted under the ground in straight lines, making sowing more efficient.

Clover

Barley

Farmers planted all their fields with different crops every year.

New crops and animals

In the 1730s Lord Townsend developed a four-field crop rotation system. This made better use of the land than the earlier three-field system (see page 16). Instead of leaving a field fallow, he planted turnips and clover. These enriched the soil and could be used to feed animals throughout the winter. As a result of this, and the growing number of enclosures, fewer animals grazed on common land. This meant that diseases did not spread as fast and animal breeding could be controlled to produce stronger, healthier animals. Two of the best known sheep and cattle breeders were Thomas Coke of Holkham in Norfolk and Robert Bakewell in Leicestershire.

In 1710 the average ox weighed 370lb. The average weight rose to 800lb in 1795.

The Commercial Revolution

By 1700 England was the most successful trading nation in Europe, with Holland as its closest rival. England traded with America, India, China, Africa and the Baltic countries. Overseas trading companies were set up, which increased England's economic and political power abroad. England also

became responsible for transporting cargo for other nations. Navigation acts were imposed in 1651, 1660 and 1663, which stated that cargoes entering or leaving English territory should only be carried in English ships, or in ships of the cargoes' country of origin. This deprived Holland of a lot of the carrying trade and made it easier for Britain to expand its commerce overseas.

An East India Company trading ship

Trading companies

Trade expanded as exploration abroad increased (see page 21). The first English trading company, the East India Company, was set up in 1600. By 1700 it controlled all British trade in India and China. During the 17th and 18th centuries other companies were established to deal with different parts of the world. These included the Hudson Bay Company (Canada) the South Sea Company (the Pacific; see page 29) and the Royal Africa Company (West Africa).

Britain exported textiles and iron goods to America, and imported raw cotton, tobacco and sugar. Timber and iron were imported from the Baltic in return for coal and manufactured goods. To the Far East Britain exported lead, silver, woollens and manufactured goods in return for silks, tea, indigo, calico, raw cotton and spices.

Britain sold over half its goods to Europe, but until 1784 it discouraged imports by imposing heavy import duties. This led to widespread smuggling* and loss of customs revenue.

Smuggling

To discourage smuggling, Robert Walpole (see page 28) established government warehouses where all imported goods had to be stored. He replaced customs duties* on items such as tea, coffee and chocolate with a tax called an excise duty.* This was paid by the consumer rather than the importer and was easier to collect. The public resented this and plans to extend the excise duties to other goods had to be abandoned. Despite these measures, smuggling was not effectively discouraged until 1784 when import duties were reduced, making smuggling less worthwhile.

The slave trade

In the 16th century Spanish, Portuguese, English and French sea-traders began to capture and sell Africans to plantation owners in South America and the West Indies who needed more labourers. By the mid-18th century Britain, Europe's major seafaring nation, was the leader in the slave trade.

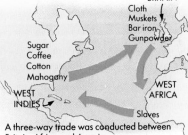

A three-way trade was conducted between Britain, Africa and America.

Ports

London was Britain's biggest port, but as trade increased other ports also became important. Liverpool and Bristol dealt with the Atlantic trade. Trade with the Baltic and the East, conducted from King's Lynn, Newcastle, Hull, Yarmouth and Ipswich, grew more slowly. After the Act of Union in 1707 (see page 25) Glasgow also became a busy port. Increased trade from the ports created wealth which merchants often invested in industries such as transport, or building.

The early 18th century

The 18th century was a time of increasing prosperity for many people in Britain. New scientific discoveries brought about improvements in agriculture and industry (see pages 26 and 34-35) which led to an increase in trade. This gave Britain the opportunity to acquire a huge overseas empire (see pages 39-41). By the end of the 18th century Britain was one of the richest and strongest powers in Europe.

King and Parliament

In 1714 George, Elector of Hanover, became George I of England. He spoke no English and left many decisions to his ministers, who became known as the Cabinet. They were usually members of the House of Lords, and chosen from the *Whig** Party, who had supported the Hanoverian claim to the throne (see page 25).

During the 18th century the power and importance of Parliament continued to grow at the expense of that of the monarch. The House of Commons had the power to suggest or *veto** legislation for new laws or taxes, and to dismiss unpopular ministers, so its support was vital to the king and Cabinet. Ministers often gained support in the Commons by bribing or making deals with MPs. In 1716 the Whigs passed the Septennial Act, which increased the government's maximum term of office from three to seven years.

Elections

The distribution of MPs dated back to the Middle Ages when each *shire**, and *borough** with a *charter** was invited to choose two MPs (see page 10). As there were more boroughs in the south than in the north, the south had more MPs. The right to vote varied from area to area but was usually based on how much property a man owned.

By the late 18th century industrial towns were growing up in the north (see page 34). However, they were not allotted more MPs to correspond with the increased population. This meant there were electoral districts in the north which had huge populations, and some in the south (known as rotten boroughs) where very few people lived.

Most MPs came from the upper classes and had rich friends who helped to get them elected. In some areas (known as pocket boroughs) elections were run by local landowners who put pressure on voters to choose a particular candidate. It is thought that over half the MPs in the Commons were elected in this way.

Robert Walpole

George I left the running of the government to his chief minister Robert Walpole. In 1732 MPs began to call him the 'Prime Minister' although the name was not officially recognized until 1905.

Walpole wanted to remain at peace with the rest of Europe, but relations with Spain and France were strained. Naval and trading rivalry led to the outbreak of war with Spain in 1739. These issues later became entangled with those of the War of the Austrian Succession (see page 30).

To encourage British trade and industry, Walpole abolished export *duties** and forbade Ireland and the American colonies to produce goods or raw materials that would compete with similar British ones. He lowered or abolished import duties on essential raw materials and made it illegal to export materials, such as wool, which were used by British manufacturers. He also tried to prevent *smuggling** (see page 27).

William Pitt, Walpole's most serious rival, entered Parliament in 1735. He and his supporters attacked Walpole's foreign policy. Walpole resigned in 1742, accused of corruption and of incompetence over Britain's role in the War of the Austrian Succession.

Parliament in 1710

Finance

Britain's first banking company, the Bank of England, was established in 1694. As trade and industry increased, many people needed to borrow large sums of money and more banks were founded. They were formed by rich individuals who lent money on condition that a rate of *interest** was paid on the loan.

£20 bank note, 1759

A system of paying debts without a direct use of cash was set up for trading purposes. Bills of exchange, which promised payment, were given in place of cash and could be exchanged for the stated sum at a bank. They worked rather like cheques do today. The introduction of shipping insurance in the 1680s also benefited traders.

The National Debt

The government first borrowed money from the Bank of England in 1694. This loan is known as the National Debt. To pay it off, a separate reserve of money called the Sinking Fund was set up in 1717. Taxation was increased to pay the interest on the debt.

In 1719 the South Sea Company (see page 27) took over the National Debt. People received shares in the company instead of the money they were owed. At first the cost of the shares rose and many people invested in them, but in 1720 the share price plummetted and investors lost a lot of money. Many politicians sold their shares before the share price fell. This led to a political scandal, which became known as the South Sea Bubble.

Non-Conformists

Parliament was still suspicious of Non-conformists (people who did not belong to the Anglican Church). Between 1711 and 1714 the *Tories** passed acts forbidding them from holding public office and from setting up their own schools. In 1719 the Whigs repealed these acts, and became popular with non-conformists as a result.

At that time the Anglican Church was becoming increasingly disorganized and corrupt. In 1729 two brothers, John and Charles Wesley, began preaching around the country. They thought the Church was failing in its duty to the poor and they preached moderation and self-denial. The Wesleys made many converts, especially in the countryside, and their followers became known as Methodists.

The Jacobite rebellions

During the 18th century there were two attempts, masterminded in Scotland, to restore the Stuart kings to the English throne. The rebels were known as Jacobites, from *Jacobus*, the Latin for James, the name of the last Stuart king (see page 25).

In 1715 rebellions were organized in Scotland and northern England in an attempt to put James II's son, James Edward, on the throne. Government troops defeated the English rebels at the Battle of Preston, and the Scots at the Battle of Sheriffmuir. A second revolt took place in 1745. This posed a greater threat to George II because England was involved in war abroad and had

fewer troops available at home. The rebels were led by James II's grandson, Charles, known as Bonnie Prince Charlie. They won the Battle of Prestonpans in 1745, and crossed the border and marched as far as Derby. However, most Englishmen were not keen to reinstate a Catholic monarch and the Jacobites failed to attract support. They retreated from Derby and were defeated at the Battle of Culloden in 1746.

English soldier

Scottish Jacobite

18th century wars

In the 18th century Britain became involved in European and colonial wars, in an attempt to maintain the *balance of power** in Europe and to protect its trading interests. Britain's major rivals were the French and the Spanish.

The War of the Spanish Succession 1702-13

The War of the Spanish Succession was fought to decide who would succeed Charles II of Spain. He died childless in 1701, having named Philip, grandson of Louis XIV of France, as heir. Austria and England feared Philip might rule both France and Spain, and supported Charles' cousin Charles, brother of Emperor Joseph of Austria.

War broke out in 1702. Fighting took place in Italy, the Netherlands, Germany and Spain. The English, led by John Churchill, 1st Duke of Marlborough, won battles at Blenheim (1704), Ramillies (1706), Oudenarde (1708), and Malplaquet (1709).

In 1711 the childless Emperor Joseph died unexpectedly and was succeeded by his brother Charles. The English withdrew their support from Charles to prevent him from ruling both Spain and Austria. They supported Philip on condition that he renounced all claim to the French throne. Peace was made in 1713. Philip became Philip V of Spain and also aquired its colonies abroad. England gained Minorca, Gibraltar, territories in America, and a share in the slave trade (see page 27). Austria gained the Spanish Netherlands.

The War of the Austrian Succession 1740-48

Emperor Charles VI of Austria died in 1740 without sons and was succeeded by his daughter Maria Theresa. Her claim to the throne was challenged by her closest male relative, Charles Albert of Bavaria. He argued that a woman should not rule the Austrian empire, and was supported by Frederick the Great of Prussia and Louis XV of France.

The War of the Austrian Succession broke out in 1740 when Prussia invaded Silesia, one of Austria's richest provinces. At the same time Austria was also at war with Spain over control of northern Italy.

England's relations with France and Spain had been strained since the 16th century when they became colonial and trading rivals (see page 21). War broke out between Britain and Spain in 1739. In 1741 Britain joined the War of the Austrian Succession by allying with Austria against France in order to protect the balance of power.

In 1742 an army, which included British troops, was formed in support of Maria Theresa and fought successfully against the French and Spanish in Italy. The army won a major victory over the French at Dettingen in Bavaria, led by George II of England (the last British monarch to go into battle).

The war ended with the Treaty of Aix-la-Chapelle in 1748. All conquered territory, except Silesia, was returned to its original owners. Britain had helped to prevent the growth of French power in Europe.

Europe 1713-14

NETHERLANDS
SPANISH NETHERLANDS
HANOVER
EAST PRUSSIA
BRITAIN
PRUSSIA
POLAND
SAXONY
PROVINCE OF SILESIA
BOHEMIA
MORAVIA
FRANCE
BAVARIA
AUSTRIA-HUNGARY
SAVOY
VENICE
SPAIN
SWITZERLAND

- England and its possessions
- Prussia and its possessions
- Austria and its possessions
- Spain and its possessions
- France and its possessions

The Seven Years' War 1756-63

The Seven Years' War was in fact two wars: the continuation of the struggle between France and Britain for control in India and North America (see page 33), and a war in Europe between Prussia and Austria. The two wars became linked when Britain allied with Prussia, and France allied with Austria.

War began in Europe when Frederick of Prussia invaded Saxony in 1756. He then invaded Bohemia but was forced to retreat in 1757. At first Britain and Prussia suffered many defeats, but in 1759 they began to have a run of victories. The British defeated the French at Minden in Germany and won control of Canada from the French at the Battle of Quebec. They also defeated the French at Quiberon Bay in West Africa and took control of the French West Indies. Although Spain joined the war in support of France in 1762, Britain and Prussia won the war later that year. By the Treaty of Paris (1763) the British gained French Canada, most territory west of the Mississippi river and nearly all the French West Indies. Britain also became the dominant European power in India, although France retained its own trading posts.

In 1763 Prussia, Austria and Saxony signed the Treaty of Hubertusburg and all European territories were restored to their pre-war owners.

The American War of Independence 1775-88

During the 17th century England founded 13 *colonies** along the eastern coast of North America. However, the colonists grew to resent British control, and this led to the American War of Independence.

In return for military protection, the colonists only traded with Britain. However, after the Seven Years' War, the government tried to impose taxes on them in order to help pay for the army in North America. The colonists argued that Britain had no right to tax them as they were not represented in Parliament. Feeling ran high and they *boycotted** British trade. In 1775 war broke out. The colonists, led by George Washington, finally defeated the British in 1781. In 1783 Britain recognized American independence.

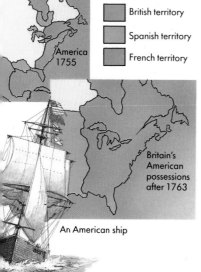

British territory

Spanish territory

America 1755

French territory

Britain's American possessions after 1763

An American ship

Key dates

1770   Boston Massacre – A British patrol fires on a crowd protesting against taxes.

1773   The Boston Tea Party – A group of Bostonians tip a cargo of British tea into Boston harbour in protest against taxation.

1775   The colonists win battles at Lexington and Concord. The British win at Bunker Hill.

1776   Representatives from each of the 13 colonies sign the Declaration of Independence.

1777   The British lose the Battle of Saratoga.

1778   France and Spain support the colonists.

1780   The British capture Charleston.

1781   Siege of Yorktown: British defeat

1783   The Treaty of Paris: Britain recognizes the independence of the 13 colonies, which are renamed the United States of America.

The later 18th century

George III (1760-1820) attempted to play a more active role in making policy. This brought him into conflict with many ministers, especially among the *Whigs**.

He wanted to end the Seven Years War with France (see page 31) because it was interrupting trade, but was opposed by the Secretary for War, William Pitt, and his supporters. However, in 1763 a group known as the 'King's Friends' bribed the Commons into giving their consent to withdrawal from the war. But Lord Bute, the Prime Minister, lost popular support over the peace treaty and resigned.

The next 20 years were dominated by problems in the American colonies (see page 31). Successive Prime Ministers resigned over colonial policy in America.

Pitt the Younger and free trade

In 1783 William Pitt the Younger was chosen by George III to be Prime Minister at the age of only 24. He aimed to improve the way Parliament was organized and to increase Britain's wealth by creating more revenue from trade. He hoped eventually to introduce free trade by abolishing import *duties**, an idea proposed by the economist Adam Smith. Smith argued that this would lower prices, encourage more trade and thereby create more wealth. Pitt believed that free trade would be especially beneficial to Britain, as it was a highly industrialized nation and likely to export more than its trading partners.

In 1786 Pitt signed a trading treaty with France which lowered some import duties. He also reorganized the revenue system, reducing the opportunity for corruption by government officials. He taxed windows and luxuries such as carriages, clocks, hair-powder and servants; reduced interest on the National Debt, and imposed an income tax to help pay for the war with France (see page 39). Some people filled in windows to avoid paying so much tax.

Parliamentary reform

When Pitt came to office, dozens of government *sinecures* (paid jobs which held no responsibility) had already been abolished. He continued this reforming policy and in 1785 put forward a bill which attempted to abolish 36 *rotten boroughs** and distribute MPs more fairly. The Commons rejected the bill.

John Wilkes and Liberty

The terms of the 1763 peace treaty (see page 31) were criticized by John Wilkes MP, in his *radical** political pamphlet, *The North Briton.* The government had him arrested but he was freed by the law courts. Parliament then *outlawed** Wilkes who fled to France. He returned in 1768 and won the election for Middlesex with the slogan "Wilkes and Liberty!" But the government denied him his parliamentary seat and this led to riots. Wilkes was finally allowed to take his seat in 1774. His case was significant because it raised questions about free speech, the freedom of the press, and people's right to choose their own MP.

Pitt and the French Revolution

After the French Revolution in 1789, there were fears that revolutionary fervour would spread to England. In 1792 the French government called for world-wide revolution.

William Pitt

In response, Pitt imposed restrictive measures to prevent the spread of revolutionary ideas. The suspension of the Habeas Corpus Act meant people could now be kept in prison without trial; the Aliens Act (1794) monitored foreigners coming into Britain, and the Seditious Practices Act (1795) made incitement to violence against the king or Parliament a *treasonable** offence. In 1795 meetings of more than 50 people were banned and a tax was imposed on newspapers. In 1799-1800 trade unions (see page 37) were also made illegal.

The British in India

Britain began trading in India in the 16th century. Its influence there increased in the 18th century. The decline of the Indian *Mogul empire** made it easier for the British to make military and trading treaties with independent local rulers.

India

Under British control from 1757

Britain was represented in India by the *East India Trading Company**. By 1763 it had defeated its French rivals with an army led by Robert Clive (known as Clive of India). After defeating the ruler of Bengal at the Battle of Plassey (1757), the Company effectively controlled the west coast of India. Its influence was so great that in 1773 the government elected a Governor-General, Warren Hastings, to regulate its work. The India Act of 1784 separated the work of trading from that of governing in India.

Canada and Australia

In 1763 Canada became a British possession. This led to friction with existing French settlers. Pitt's Canada Act (1791) attempted to reduce this by splitting Canada into two provinces, each ruled by a governor and a legislative council: Upper Canada for the British colonists and Lower Canada for the French. However, the French and British *colonists** both resented this.

Australia and New Zealand were first discovered by the Dutch in the 17th century. However, from 1768 to 1779 James Cook explored their coasts and *annexed** them for Britain. Australia began as a convict colony; the first convicts landed in 1788. However, free settlers followed and by 1830 they outnumbered the convicts.

Captain Cook was killed in Hawaii in 1779.

Ireland

In 1790 an Irish Protestant called Wolfe Tone set up the Society of United Irishmen which campaigned for Irish independence and equal rights for Catholics and Protestants. Some anti-Catholic laws were repealed in 1793.

In 1796 the Society asked the French government for military help against the British. The French sent a fleet to Ireland in 1796 but bad weather stopped it landing. In January 1798 two French forces landed but they were defeated and forced to surrender. Wolfe Tone was captured and sentenced to death. A second rebellion in June was crushed by the British at Vinegar Hill.

Pitt feared that if he granted Irish independence the country might be used as a base for attacks on Britain. By offering *peerages** and bribes, he persuaded the Irish Parliament to agree to its own abolition. By the Act of Union (1801), Ireland became part of the United Kingdom of Great Britain and Ireland; 100 Irish MPs were elected to the Commons and 32 peers entered the Lords. The Anglican Church became the official Irish Church. Most Irish people opposed union. Although 88% of them were Catholic, Catholics were still not allowed to sit in Parliament. Pitt tried to give Catholics greater political freedom, but George III refused and Pitt resigned as a result.

Key dates

1701-13	War of Spanish Succession
1715	Jacobite Rebellion
1720	The South Sea Bubble
1740-48	War of Austrian Succession
1745	Jacobite Rebellion
1756-63	The Seven Years' War
1757	Clive wins the Battle of Plassey.
1768-79	Cook explores Australia.
1775-83	American War of Independence
1789	French Revolution
1798	Irish rebellion
1801	Union with Ireland

33

The Industrial Revolution

By the 18th century Britain was a rich nation. Its wealth was mainly derived from farming and the woollen cloth trade. However, from the 1750s the introduction of new inventions and the discovery of steam as a source of power led to the development of industry. Steam-power revolutionized transport (see below) and altered the production of coal and cloth. It also made possible the growth of new industries, such as steel.

The use of new, power-driven machines meant that cloth could no longer be produced in workers' homes and so factories were built. Towns grew up around the factories and people moved from the country to live and work in them. By the mid-19th century towns were over crowded, unhealthy places.

This rapid industrial change is known as the Industrial Revolution, and Britain was the first country to experience it.

Wool and cotton cloth

The Spinning Jenny spun 16 wool threads at once instead of just one.

Cotton cloth, first imported into Britain from the Far East in about 1680, became popular. Cottage workers in England began to spin their own cotton thread but it was very weak.

Wool production was improved by new machines such as John Kay's Flying Shuttle (1733)† and James Hargreaves' Spinning Jenny (1767). Machines such as Richard Arkwright's Water Frame (1769) and Samuel Crompton's Mule (1779) improved cotton manufacture, by producing strong, thin, cotton thread. The Water Frame was powered by large amounts of water and so could not be used in a domestic setting. In 1771 Arkwright set up the world's first cotton factory in Derbyshire. From the mid-1780s, cotton textile machinery was run increasingly on steam power. From 1800 cotton manufacture became Britain's leading industry.

Coal

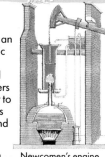

Newcomen's engine

Coal was already an important domestic fuel. As industries grew, the demand increased, so miners had to dig deeper to find more of it. This was dangerous and many workers (including women and children) died as a result of flooding, explosive gases and lack of oxygen. In 1706 Thomas Newcomen invented the first practical working steam engine. It pumped water from below 90m (300ft) and prevented serious floods. A similar but more efficient engine was designed in 1769 by James Watt. During the 18th century Britain's annual coal output quadrupled and inventions, such as Humphrey Davy's safety lamp, improved conditions.

Iron and steel

Iron is produced by heating iron ore. Until the 18th century, very little iron was produced. Charcoal (carbonized wood) was used as fuel, but it was scarce. Coal, the alternative fuel, made the iron brittle. In 1709 Abraham Darby found a way to produce a better quality iron, called cast iron, using coke (carbonized coal). Coke-fuelled furnaces became common and iron production moved from forests to coal-mining areas. In 1784 Henry Cort developed a technique called puddling to produce wrought iron (which is easier to shape than cast iron).

Steel (iron with carbon added) was first produced in the 1740s by Benjamin Huntsman. It was stronger than wrought iron, and production was improved by the introduction of Henry Bessemer's Converter (1856). Between 1850 and 1880 Britain's annual steel output tripled. Steel became important in structural engineering. Ships were now made of iron or steel (instead of wood) and were steam-driven. The first steam-driven Atlantic crossing was made in 1838 by the Great Western, a ship designed by Isambard Brunel.

† Dates given for inventions refer to the year of patent*.

Transport

As industrial production grew, it became vital to find a cheap way of transporting heavy loads. To fulfil this need, canals were built linking most industrial areas and sea ports, and roads were improved. Cheap transport meant that goods became less expensive.

In the 19th century steam trains (adapted from Watt's engine) were introduced. At first they were only used to carry coal, but by the 1840s Britain had a complex passenger railway system. The railways superseded canals as cheap transport and boosted the iron and coal industries by creating revenue from carrying freight and passengers.

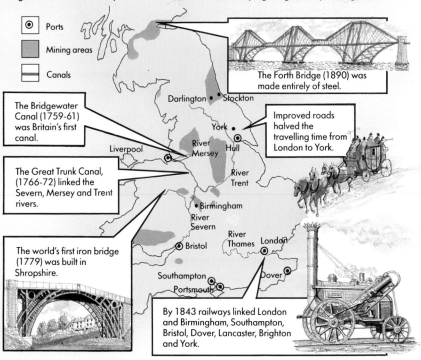

Ports

Mining areas

Canals

Darlington • Stockton

The Bridgewater Canal (1759-61) was Britain's first canal.

York

Liverpool

River Mersey

Hull

The Great Trunk Canal, (1766-72) linked the Severn, Mersey and Trent rivers.

River Trent

The world's first iron bridge (1779) was built in Shropshire.

• Birmingham

River Severn

River Thames London

Bristol

Southampton

Portsmouth

Dover

The Forth Bridge (1890) was made entirely of steel.

Improved roads halved the travelling time from London to York.

By 1843 railways linked London and Birmingham, Southampton, Bristol, Dover, Lancaster, Brighton and York.

Key dates

1705 Thomas Newcomen's piston steam engine

1733 John Kay's Flying Shuttle

1767 James Hargreaves' Spinning Jenny

1769 Richard Arkwright's Water Frame

1779 Samuel Crompton's Mule

1782 James Watt's rotary steam engine

1788 William Symington builds Britain's first steam-powered ship.

1804 Richard Trevithick builds the first steam train to run along a track.

1825 The Stockton to Darlington line (Britain's first public railway) is opened.

1829 Stephenson's steam train, the Rocket, reaches a top speed of 30mph.

1856 Henry Bessemer's steel converter

1863 Opening of the London Underground

1890 First electric underground train

1897 Charles Peterson's steam turbine engine increases speed and fuel efficiency.

19th century home affairs

The 19th century was a time of great economic and political change in Britain. The country was becoming industrialized (see pages 34-35) and overseas trade was increasing. By the mid-century Britain was known as the 'workshop of the world'. Abroad, Britain built up a huge empire (see pages 39-41).

The Crystal Palace in London was originally built in 1851 for the first international trade fair, and later enlarged.

At home, the working classes were demanding a better standard of living and the right to vote and stand in parliamentary elections. There were increasing problems in Ireland.

Political groups

At the beginning of the century there were three political groups: the *Whigs**, the *Tories** and the *Radicals**. Until 1858 all MPs had to be property owners (and before 1911 they were unpaid). As a result Parliament was dominated by the upper classes. The working classes could not vote and had limited political power. Only the Radicals campaigned for widespread social and electoral reform. Most Tories wanted the parliamentary system to stay as it was, and the Whigs only supported moderate change. In the second half of the century two new parties appeared: the Liberal Party (see opposite) and the Independent Labour Party, which was set up by and for the working classes.

Social unrest

Early in the century wars in Europe and the United States disrupted trade. The growing use of machinery in the cloth trade led to unemployment among workers and kept wages low.

As a result there were riots and public demonstrations. Some rioters claimed to be led by a man named Nedd Ludd, and became known as Luddites. They destroyed machinery, which led the Tory government to pass laws against political meetings and propaganda.

The Corn Laws

Public unrest was made worse by the introduction of the Corn Laws in 1815. To help British farmers, the government banned the import of corn (cereals) until British corn reached a certain price. The price of corn and bread (a major part of most people's diets) therefore remained high. The Anti-Corn Law League, led by by a Radical MP, Richard Cobden, campaigned for the repeal of the Corn Laws. The Tories, led by Robert Peel, repealed them in 1846.

The Liberal Party

The repeal of the Corn Laws led to a split in the Tory party (often known as the *Conservative** Party after 1834). The majority followed Benjamin Disraeli and Lord Derby. The rest, known as Peelites, joined some Whigs and Radicals, and in 1859 formed the Liberal Party. The Liberals were led by William Gladstone from 1868 to 1894.

Gladstone

Disraeli

Law and order reforms

Early in the century high unemployment led to an increase in crime. Although over 120 crimes were punishable by death, this failed to act as a deterrent. There was no organized police force and criminals were rarely caught. In 1823 Robert Peel (then Tory Home Secretary) abolished the death penalty for over 100 crimes. He introduced reforms aimed at improving the crowded and unhealthy conditions in prisons. In 1829 he founded the Metropolitan Police Force.

The first reform bill

The demand for electoral reform increased. A reform bill was passed in 1832 by the Whig government, but it was based on property, so it only extended the vote to the middle classes.

As a result, more *pressure groups** were set up to campaign for further reform. A group called the Chartists (so-called because they presented petitions called charters to Parliament) campaigned for the right of every man to vote and stand in parliamentary elections.

The Houses of Parliament were rebuilt between 1840 and 1860, following a fire in 1834.

Trade unions

The first trade unions were organized locally and began as a way for workers to bargain with their employers over pay, and living and working conditions.

Fearing that unions would encourage violence, Parliament made them illegal in 1799-1800. However, unions were legalized in 1824 after campaigns by Radical MPs.

The first national union, the Grand National Consolidated Trade Union (GNCTU), was set up in 1833 by the Radical MP and mill-owner Robert Owen. He hoped a strong national union would be able to pressurize the government into passing more social and factory reform laws (see below). The union met with opposition and employers often threatened to dismiss employees if they joined.

In 1834 six men from Tolpuddle in Dorset were deported to Australia for trying to set up a local branch. They became known as the Tolpuddle Martyrs. The GNCTU collapsed and workers turned to other forms of political activity such as Chartism.

Unions and the TUC

During the 1850s small unions of skilled workers from individual crafts were set up. These were known as model unions. Union officials from each area began to meet to discuss problems and in 1868 they formed the Trades Union Congress (TUC). The TUC acted as a means of influencing leading politicians. In 1869 a government report stated that strong unions seemed to reduce violence by workers rather than increase it. As a result, the government relaxed some of the anti-trade union laws. Unions of unskilled workers were formed during the 1880s.

Electoral reform and the Labour Party

In 1867 all male householders in towns became eligible to vote and stand for Parliament. This added over a million voters to the electorate. In 1884 this was extended to all male householders and in 1918 to all men over 21.

In 1874 Thomas Burt and Alexander Macdonald became the first working class MPs. In 1893 the Independent Labour Party was formed by Keir Hardie, an MP and miners' leader. In 1900 the Labour Representation Committee was set up. It was renamed the Labour Party in 1906.

Factory reform

From early in the 19th century reformers campaigned to improve the poor pay, long hours and unhealthy conditions in factories and mines, and to ban the employment of young children. By the end of the century a lower age limit of 11 had been set. Rules were laid down to regulate working conditions and factories were subject to inspection.

Education

Before 1833 schools were funded by rich individuals or the Church, rather than the State, and often had to charge fees as well. As a result few poor children went to school. However, from 1833 the government gave grants to some schools. In 1870 the first board schools were set up for poor children, paid for out of public money. Education to the age of 11 was made compulsory in 1881, and became free in 1891. Grant-funded secondary schools called grammar schools were introduced in 1902.

Public health

Health care also slowly improved. From 1700 to 1825 over 150 hospitals were set up, chiefly financed by rich benefactors. The first hospitals were unhygienic and patients often died from infection or shock after operations. But

in 1846 Joseph Lister pioneered the use of antiseptics, and in 1847 James Simpson first used chloroform as an anaesthetic. In 1853 Florence Nightingale set up the first training school for nurses at St Thomas's Hospital, London.

Victorian nurses

The first Public Health Act was passed in 1848. The next major acts, in 1872 and 1875, compelled local authorities to appoint health officers and to improve water supplies and sanitary conditions.

Catholics and Ireland

In 1828 Daniel O' Connell, an Irish Catholic, stood for and won the election for County Clare in Ireland. As Catholics were not allowed to vote or hold public office, Parliament refused to let him take his seat. This led to violence in Ireland. Fearing an Irish civil war, Parliament gave Catholics the right to vote in 1829. This is known as the Catholic Emancipation Act.

Charles Parnell

Most large landowners in Ireland were English. The native Irish were usually very poor and farming methods were inadequate to feed the growing population. Between 1846 and 1848 the failure of the potato crop (the staple Irish food) led to famine and over a million people died. Many blamed the English and groups such as the Fenians formed to press for Irish *Home Rule**.

Between 1869 and 1874 the Liberals passed several acts to improve the Irish situation. They tried to increase the legal rights of tenant farmers and repealed the law which had established the Anglican Church as the official Irish Church. The *Tory** government of 1874-80 refused to make reforms. In 1879 the Irish Land League was formed to press for land reform. It was led by Charles Parnell, a campaigner for Home Rule. In 1886 and 1893 the Liberals tried and failed to pass Irish Home Rule bills.

Key dates: home affairs

1811 The Prince of Wales becomes Prince *Regent**.

1811-17 Luddite riots

1816 Riots at Spa Fields in London

1817 Uprisings in Derbyshire

1819 Peterloo massacre – demonstrators at St Peter's field, Manchester, are charged by mounted soldiers.

1820-30 Reign of George IV

1829 Catholic Emancipation Act

1830-37 Reign of William IV

1832 The Great Reform Bill

1833 Parliament passes William Wilberforce's bill to abolish slavery in the British empire (see page 31).

1837-1901 Reign of Queen Victoria (shown below), Britain's longest reigning monarch

1840 The Penny Post, Britain's first postal service, is introduced.

1846-48 Irish potato famines

1851 The Great Exhibition

1867 Reform Bill

Queen Victoria

19th century foreign affairs

From the late 18th century Britain extended its control into India, China, the Middle East and Africa, and slowly built up an empire overseas. The need to protect or extend its territorial and trading interests meant that Britain was often involved in wars in these areas.

In the first half of the century foreign policy was directed by the Foreign Secretary. The most important were Canning, Castlereagh, and Palmerston. From about 1860 the Prime Minister took more interest in foreign policy.

Both the Liberal and Tory parties aimed to safeguard the empire. Although Gladstone criticized Disraeli's policies, he pursued similar ones himself when in office.

War with France

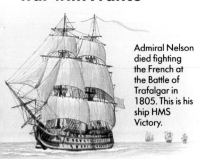

Admiral Nelson died fighting the French at the Battle of Trafalgar in 1805. This is his ship HMS Victory.

In the French Revolution of 1789-92 the French overthrew their monarchy and replaced it with a *republic**. Other European countries feared the spread of revolutionary ideas, and in 1793 Britain became allied with Austria and Prussia for a war against France. In 1796 and 1797 the French, led by Napoleon Bonaparte, seized parts of Belgium and Italy from Austria.

Napoleon aimed to extend French influence throughout the world. He planned to conquer the rest of Europe first, followed by India, the Middle East and the Caribbean. The British navy, led by Admiral Horatio Nelson, put a stop to Napoleon's ambitions in the East when they defeated him at the Battle of the Nile in Egypt in 1799.

In 1803 Napoleon seized Switzerland and more of Italy and in 1804 he became Emperor of France.

He planned to invade Britain after first destroying its navy. However, in 1805 Nelson defeated the French fleet at the Battle of Trafalgar, off the south coast of Spain. Despite this setback, Napoleon won more victories against the Austrians and the Russians, and took control of Germany.

In 1808 Napoleon invaded Spain and Portugal, hoping to isolate Britain from its European trading partners. However, with British support, the Spaniards and Portuguese gradually drove out the French. The British troops were led by Sir Arthur Wellesley (who became the Duke of Wellington).

In 1812 Napoleon failed to conquer Russia, and in 1813 Austrian, Prussian and Russian forces won major battles against him in Germany. Britain invaded France in 1814 and Napoleon was deposed and exiled. He raised a new army in 1815, but was beaten at the Battle of Waterloo by the British (led by Wellington), the Prussians and the Belgians. Peace was made at the Congress of Vienna in 1815.

India

After 1784 India was administered by a number of Governor Generals who extended British control. Many Indians resented British interference in their social and religious customs and in 1857 Indian soldiers mutinied against their British officers. The rebellion, known as the Indian Mutiny, spread throughout northern and central India and was finally suppressed in 1858. The same year the *East India Company** was abolished and its lands taken over by the British government. In 1876 Queen Victoria became Empress of India, and India was governed by her representative, the Viceroy.

The fort at Agra in northern India

The Eastern Question

The Ottoman empire was established by Turkish *Muslims** in the 13th century and expanded to cover large parts of Europe, Africa and the Middle East. But from the 1680s it proved too big to control. Political problems arose as the empire began to weaken and subject peoples started to press for freedom.

Many European nations feared their rivals might increase their power by acquiring former Ottoman territory. Britain became involved in war in the Crimea (see below) to prevent Russian expansion into Turkey. In 1878 Russia threatened to invade Afghanistan. Believing that the Russians might cross into India, Britain sent troops to bring Afghanistan under British control.

Ottoman territory 1683

CRIMEA
RUSSIA
Black Sea
TURKEY
AFGHANISTAN
INDIA

The Crimean War

In 1853 Russia claimed the right to protect all *Christians** in the Ottoman empire. Turkey refused and Russia then invaded Turkish lands. Britain and France did not want Russia to extend its influence, and in September 1854 they besieged Russia's naval base at Sebastopol in the Crimea. By November they had won three major battles — Alma, Balaclava and Inkerman.

However, British military organization was poor. At Balaclava, the Light Horse Brigade, armed only with swords, was ordered to charge at the Russian canons. Out of 673 men, 247 died.

The Charge of the
Light Brigade

The army suffered many hardships in the Crimea including shortages of medicine, food, and clothing. The reports of the Times war correspondent W.H. Russell roused public opinion. Medical conditions were improved by a team of nurses led by Florence Nightingale.

In 1855 the British took Sebastopol and the war ended in 1856.

The Opium Wars

In the 18th century China limited its trade with other countries, and only took silver as payment for its exports (chiefly tea, porcelain and silk). However, early in the 19th century, British merchants persuaded Chinese traders to accept opium, an Indian drug, as payment. (The British government had banned the opium trade in India, and traders wanted to sell it elsewhere.)

The Chinese government resented the loss in silver payments and feared the results of importing an addictive drug. In 1839 they seized all the opium in Canton. Britain sent gun-boats and war broke out. In 1842 a peace treaty was drawn up by which the Chinese gave control of Hong Kong to the British†. But tension remained and in 1857 war began again. After the British attacked Canton, the Chinese surrendered and were forced to open all their ports to European trade.

Chinese
porcelain

Egypt

The Suez Canal, which links the Red Sea and the Mediterranean Sea, was built by France and Egypt in 1869. In 1875 Britain bought Egypt's shares. The canal was a major boost to British trade because it cut the journey from Britain to India by 4000 miles.

Keen to protect their interests in the canal, the British became concerned with the political affairs of Egypt and its neighbour, the Sudan (which had been under Egyptian control since 1821).

† *China resumes control in 1997.*

40

The Sudan

In 1881 Britain sent troops to Egypt to suppress an uprising. In 1883 there was a rebellion in the Sudan against Egyptian control, led by the Sudanese religious leader, the Mahdi. A British force, led by General Charles Gordon, was sent to evacuate the Egyptians there. Against orders he established his troops in the capital Khartoum, and fought the rebels. The rebels besieged Khartoum and many British soldiers died, including Gordon. Gladstone sent troops but they arrived too late. As a result, he lost popular support and had to resign. In 1896 his successor, Lord Salisbury, sent troops to retake the Sudan. In 1898 the British, led by Lord Kitchener, defeated the Khalifa, the Mahdi's successor, at the Battle of Omdurman and established Anglo-Egyptian control of Sudan.

War and expansion in southern Africa

In 1652 the Dutch set up Cape Colony, the first European *colony** in southern Africa. Other Europeans began to settle there in the 18th century, which led to tension. In 1815 Britain took control of Cape Colony. The Dutch settlers, known as Boers, resented this and in 1836 many left and set up two new colonies, the Orange Free State and the Transvaal.

In the 1870s the Transvaal Boers were threatened by a native people, the Zulus. In 1877 the Boers allowed the British to *annex** the Transvaal in return for protection. In 1879 war broke out

between the British and the Zulus, which ended in Zulu defeat. The Boers demanded their land back and in 1881 the First Boer War broke out. It ended with a British defeat at Majuba Hill. In 1884 Britain granted independence to the Transvaal. After the Second Boer War (1899-1901) the Transvaal and the Orange Free State became part of the British Empire.

Zulu warrior

The Scramble for Africa

At the beginning of the 19th century, most of Africa was unknown to Europeans. However, awareness of Africa's vast natural resources, which included gold and diamonds, increased during the 1870s. As a result, several countries tried to establish colonies there. By 1914 most of Africa had been colonized by Britain, France, Belgium, Germany and Portugal. The process was so rapid it became known as the Scramble for Africa.

Key dates : foreign policy

1793-1815   War with France

1812-14   War with America

1839-42   The First Opium War with China

1854-56   Crimean War

1857   Indian Mutiny

1858   India comes under British government control.

1875   Britain buys Suez canal shares.

1876   Victoria becomes Empress of India.

1877   Britain annexes the Transvaal.

1881   First Boer War

1883-85   Rebellion in the Sudan

1899-1902   Second Boer War

1900   The Boxer Rebellion in China — Chinese *nationalists** attack and lay siege to Europeans in Peking.

World War I 1914-18

World War I was a European war, although fighting also took place in Turkey, the Middle East and in the *colonies** of the European powers. Over 17 million people were killed.

At the start of the 20th century relations between the European powers were strained. Britain felt threatened by Germany's growing naval and economic power. France resented Germany's victory in the Franco-Prussian War in 1871. Germany feared being encircled by hostile countries. Austria-Hungary and Russia disputed who should have most influence in the Balkans (which bitterly resented outside interference).

A war poster 1914

Rival alliances grew up. Germany and Austria-Hungary (known as the Central Powers) were on one side, and France, Britain and Russia, (known as the Allies) on the other.

YOUR COUNTRY NEEDS YOU

How the war started

In June 1914, Franz Ferdinand, the Austro-Hungarian heir, was assassinated in Sarajevo, in Bosnia (a Balkan state) by a Serbian *nationalist**.

Archduke Franz Ferdinand

This led Austria to threaten Serbia with war unless it submitted to Austrian rule. Serbia refused and Austria declared war. Russia supported Serbia and *mobilized** against Austria. Germany (Austria's ally) then declared war on Russia and its ally France. Germany tried to attack France by marching through Belgium (a *neutral** country since 1839). On 4 August Britain joined the war in defence of Belgium.

The Central Powers were joined by Turkey (1914) and Bulgaria (1915). The Allies were joined by Italy (1915), Romania (1916) and the USA (1917).

The course of the war

The Western Front
The Germans fought the British and the French on the Western Front. From 1915 to spring 1918 there was a *stalemate** in which millions of men died and neither side gained much territory.

The Eastern Front
Germany planned to invade France and then Russia. But Russia attacked first, forcing Germany to fight on two fronts at once. Russia lost a great deal of territory and withdrew from the war after the Russian Revolution in 1917.

The Middle East
The Allies attacked Turkey and Salonika (in Greece) in an attempt to break the stalemate in the West. Although they did not succeed, by 1918, they controlled parts of Iran and Iraq and most of Palestine and Syria.

BRITAIN 1914
BELGIUM 1914
Western front 1914-17
GERMANY 1914
Eastern front 1917
Eastern Front 1914
RUSSIA 1914
FRANCE 1914
AUSTRIA-HUNGARY 1914
SWITZERLAND
ROMANIA 1916
BULGARIA 1915
PORTUGAL 1916
ITALY 1915
1916
SPAIN
Gallipoli
SERBIA 1914
TURKEY 1914
GREECE 1915
1917

Neutral countries
Central Powers and date of entry into war
Allies and date of entry into war
Allied territory occupied by Central Powers and date occupied
Central power territory occupied by the Allies and date occupied

War at sea

From the start of the war, Britain blockaded German sea ports to cut off supplies to Germany. From 1915 the Germans used submarines called U-boats to attack British ships. In response Britain used a convoy system of warships to protect its own supply vessels. This helped to lessen British losses.

In 1915 the Lusitania, a ship with American and British civilians on board, was sunk by the Germans on the grounds that it was carrying weapons. Continued German U-boat attacks on armed and unarmed ships provoked America into declaring war on Germany in April 1917.

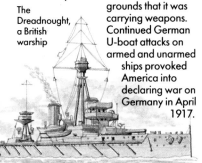

The Dreadnought, a British warship

Methods of warfare

Military technology had improved since the 19th century. Explosive mines, poison mustard gas, tanks and better machine-guns were all introduced. At first aeroplanes were used to locate the enemy, and after 1917 both sides had bomber planes. Germany bombed London in 1917. Britain retaliated in 1918.

Trench warfare

War in Europe was fought from a system of ditches called trenches, protected by barbed wire and machine-guns. However, successful attack was almost impossible, as each side could fire on enemy attacks from the protection of their own trenches. The situation changed in 1918 when the Allies introduced tanks on a large scale, making attack easier.

A British trench

The home front

For Britain, it was the first time that civilians were actively involved in the war effort. From 1916 all able-bodied men aged between 18 and 41 had to go into the army and women replaced them in their jobs. Civilians were also affected by shortages and from 1917 food was rationed.

The last years of the war

When Russia withdrew from the war in 1917, the Germans moved all their forces to the Western Front. In spring 1918 they advanced on Paris, but were halted by the Allies and gradually pushed back. Meanwhile Austria was defeated in Italy, and Bulgaria and Turkey lost ground in Salonika and the Middle East.

In November 1918 the German army was defeated and its navy mutinied. This led to a revolution, and the formation of the German *Republic**. On 11 November the Germans surrendered. By the Treaty of Versailles Germany had to admit guilt for the war. The Allies claimed huge financial compensation, confiscated territory and forbade the Germans from stationing troops near the River Rhine, close to Germany's borders with western Europe.

Key dates

1914 *June* Archduke Franz Ferdinand is murdered; *July* Austria declares war on Serbia; *August* Germany declares war on France and Russia; *September* The Battle of the Marne – Allied troops halt Germany's invasion of France.

1915 Allies retreat after defeat at Gallipoli – 205,000 Allied casualties; Italy joins Allies; Bulgaria joins Germany.

1916 Romania joins Allies; *February – June* Battle of Verdun – longest battle of the war lasting 300 days; *July – November* Battle of the Somme – 600,000 Allied casualties

1917 Russia withdraws from the war; USA joins the Allies; Battle of Ypres (also called Passchendaele)

1918 *November* German navy surrenders.

1919 Treaty of Versailles

Social and political change 1900-1939

The Liberal government of 1906 to 1915 introduced measures to improve the lives of children, the sick, the elderly and the unemployed. Between 1906 and 1909 free school meals and medical services and an old age pension scheme were introduced. The Workmen's Compensation Act of 1906 gave compensation for industrial accidents and in 1911 a National Insurance scheme was set up to cover medical care for employees. These reforms were paid for out of increased income tax.

Trade unions

Trade unions (see page 37) gradually gained power. They bargained for

better pay and conditions, often using the threat of strikes. In 1901 the Taff Vale Railway Company successfully sued the railway union for loss of revenue during a strike. This ruling threatened the future of strike action,

A union banner 1913

but was reversed in 1906. Several strikes took place between 1910 and 1912, but once war broke out in 1914 (see pages 42-43) there were fewer strikes.

Government after World War I

During World War I (see pages 42-43) the Labour Party grew in popularity. It came to power for the first time in 1924 and again in 1929. In 1931 there were serious economic problems (see below) and the Prime Minister, Ramsay MacDonald, cut public benefits. This was against Labour policy and led to the resignation of most of MacDonald's government.

MacDonald then formed a *coalition** with the leader of the Conservatives, Stanley Baldwin, known as the National Government. Although it was unpopular with Labour and Liberal MPs, the coalition was returned to power in 1935.

Industrial crisis

Between 1919 and 1921, British trade abroad increased. But many countries began to develop their own industries or look for new trading partners (such as America) and Britain began to lose business. This led to high unemployment and low wages, especially in industries such as iron, steel and coal. By 1921 unemployment had risen to two million.

The General Strike

In 1926 the miners went on strike because they were being threatened with longer hours and a cut in wages. The Trades Union Congress (TUC) succeeded in calling upon other industries to strike in sympathy. This all-out stoppage, called the General Strike, lasted nine days. The miners continued their strike for a year but eventually had to accept the new terms. In 1927 the government passed the Trades Disputes Act making sympathy strikes illegal.

The Great Depression

The world economy deteriorated in the 1930s. This was due to a number of factors, including the effects of the World War I and the failure of the American money market in 1929 (known as the Wall Street Crash). All countries which traded with America were affected; businesses were ruined and there was huge unemployment. By 1935 the situation in Britain began to improve, especially in the south and in the Midlands where new industries such as car manufacture were being set up. Northern areas which relied on heavy industry, such as Jarrow (see date box), recovered more slowly.

Women Fight for Rights

Before the 20th century women had very few legal rights. Until 1882 a woman's property automatically became her husband's on marriage.

In 1903 the Women's Social and Political Union was set up by Emmeline and Christabel Pankhurst. They campaigned for women's rights, and above all for the right to vote in parliamentary elections. Women who campaigned for the vote were known as Suffragettes. It was a long struggle and some women went to prison for their political activities. The important role of women in the war effort (taking over the jobs done by men who had gone to fight) made women's demands less easy to refuse, and in 1919 women over the age of 30 were finally given the vote. In 1928 the age limit was lowered to 21, the same as for men.

Ireland

Tension continued in Ireland over the problem of Home Rule (see page 38). In the British general election of 1910 the Liberals won only two seats more than the Conservatives. Both parties therefore needed the support of the 82 Irish MPs in order to have a working majority. The Irish agreed to support the Liberals in return for Irish Home Rule. A bill was passed giving a Dublin government full control, except over foreign and constitutional matters. It was due to become law in August 1914.

However, the bill was shelved after Irish Protestants (who lived mainly in the north) refused to be ruled by the Catholic majority in the south. Supported by the Conservatives, the Protestants set up a private army, the Ulster Volunteers. In response the Catholics formed the Nationalist Volunteers.

Civil war seemed imminent but was averted by the start of the World War I. Although it had been agreed that hostilities should be suspended, there was a revolt in Dublin in 1916, known as the Easter Rising. The British crushed the rebellion, and executed 16 rebel leaders.

After the war, the British government tried to solve the problem by dividing Ireland into two zones, the northern part for Protestants and the southern part for Catholics. This led to unrest in the south because many Catholics wanted Ireland united under Home Rule. In 1921 Home Rule was granted to Southern Ireland. The north remained part of Great Britain, with limited self-government through the Northern Irish Assembly at Stormont. This angered the south and led to more violence which lasted until 1923.

In 1937 Southern Ireland became a *sovereign state** and was renamed Eire. Eire now ruled itself, under President Eamon de Valera, although the British monarch was still *head of state**.

Flag of Southern Ireland

Northern Ireland

Eire

Flag of Northern Ireland

Key dates

1914-18 World War I

1919 Votes granted to women over 30

1921 Home Rule for Southern Ireland

1926 General Strike; *Dominion** status granted to Canada, New Zealand, South Africa, Australia and Southern Ireland.

1928 Votes for women aged over 21

1929 Wall Street Crash

1936 Jarrow Crusade – the unemployed of Jarrow march to London to protest; Edward VIII *abdicates** to marry Wallis Simpson, an American divorcee.

1937 Southern Ireland becomes sovereign state of Eire.

World War II 1939-45

In the 1930s German military strength grew under the Nazis (National Socialists), led by Adolf Hitler. This threatened the *balance of power** in Europe.

In 1938 Hitler enforced a union with Austria and marched into part of Czechoslovakia. Britain and France wanted to avoid war and at a meeting in Munich they agreed to allow Hitler to keep these territories. However, Hitler then *annexed** the rest of Czechoslovakia and seemed to be threatening Poland. In March 1939 Britain agreed to support Poland in the event of a German invasion. On 1 September Germany invaded Poland. Britain and France (known as the Allied Powers) declared war two days later. Italy allied with Germany in 1940 and Japan followed in 1941. They became known as the Axis Powers. The USSR and the USA joined the Allies in 1941.

Britain sent troops to France, but at the start of the war fighting only took place in the Atlantic and Indian Oceans. The land battle began in April 1940. Over a period of seven weeks, Germany invaded and conquered Norway, Denmark, Holland, Belgium, Luxemburg and France. Dive-bombers, tanks and paratroopers were used in the invasions. This became known as *Blitzkrieg*, meaning 'lightning war'. The British army was forced to retreat and by 24 May was trapped in northern France. Over nine days, 340,000 men were rescued by British naval and civilian ships from the beaches of Dunkirk.

The Battle of Britain

The Germans bombed British ports, cities, airfields and factories in preparation for an invasion. The Battle of Britain, a series of battles to establish air supremacy, was fought between 15 August and 15 September 1940. German losses were huge and plans to invade Britain were abandoned.

Spitfire

Bombing raids

Hurricane

After the Battle of Britain, German bombers began night-time raids on Britain. This was known as the *Blitz* and continued until the spring of 1941. In response, Britain and the USA (who had joined the war in December 1941) heavily bombed targets in Germany and German occupied countries. A second *blitz* took place between 1944 and 1945 when Germany bombed the south of England with new flying bombs called V1s and V2s.

During air-raids many people in London sheltered in underground stations.

The Eastern Front

The USSR joined the war in June 1941, after Germany attacked and captured many Soviet provinces. The German army failed to reach Moscow before winter and so headed south. However, it was forced to retreat after a major battle near Stalingrad (September 1942- January 1943). By spring 1944 Soviet forces had regained most of the land they had lost. They marched west, liberating German occupied countries such as Poland and Hungary. In 1945 they invaded Germany itself.

War in North Africa

War in North Africa began in June 1940 when the Italians and Germans attacked the British army in Egypt. In 1942 the British, led by Field Marshall Montgomery, won a decisive victory over the Germans, led by Field Marshall Rommel, at the Battle of El Alamein. The Germans retreated and became trapped in Tunisia between the British in the east and Allied troops advancing in the west. In May 1943 the German army in North Africa surrendered. The Allies then invaded Sicily and Italy. Italy surrendered in September 1943.

British troops in North Africa.

Civilian lives

The war directly affected the lives of civilians. Bombing raids killed 60,000 people in Britain and 600,000 in Germany. The Nazis also imprisoned and exterminated millions of people whom they saw as undesirable. This applied mainly to Jews; other victims included *radicals** and homosexuals. This is known as the *Holocaust*.

In Britain, children were sent to safety in the country. Most men were at war, so women did their jobs. Rationing was introduced because items were scarce. A civilian defence army, the Home Guard, was set up for use in the event of invasion. By 1941 over 1.5 million people had joined volunteer groups to help the war effort.

The end of the war in Europe

On 6 June, 1944 the Allies landed in Normandy in northern France and the Germans were forced to retreat. This is known as D-Day. On 24 March 1945 the Allies crossed the River Rhine. On 2 May they met up with the Russian army who were advancing from the opposite direction. Germany surrendered on 8 May 1945 and the war in Europe ended.

Winston Churchill, Britain's Prime Minister 1940-1945

War in the Pacific

War began in the Pacific in December 1941, when the Japanese bombed the American naval base at Pearl Harbour in Hawaii. They immediately attacked Malaya (a British colony) and by June 1942 controlled most of the Pacific.

Japanese expansion was halted in spring 1942 after they suffered defeats in the Coral Sea and Midway. American forces slowly retook small islands and from them launched aerial attacks. Eventually they were close enough to bomb Tokyo. To end the war with Japan, the USA dropped atom bombs on the cities of Hiroshima and Nagasaki in August 1945. Japan surrendered on 14 August and on 2 September 1945 signed the *armistice** which ended the war.

American flag

Japanese flag

Key dates

1939 *1 September* Germans invade Poland; *3 September* Britain and France declare war on Germany.

1940 *May* Dunkirk evacuation; *June* Italy joins Germany; *August-October* Battle of Britain

1941 *June* Germans invade USSR; *December* Pearl Harbour; America and Japan join the war.

1942 *October* Battle of El Alamein

1944 *6 June* D-Day

1945 *January-March* Allies invade Germany; *30 April* Hitler commits suicide; *8 May* Germany surrenders; *August* USA drops atom bombs on Hiroshima and Nagasaki; *14 August* Japan surrenders.
  November 1945 – October 1946 The Nuremburg Trials – 24 Nazi leaders are tried by the Allies as war criminals. Only three are acquitted.

Britain after 1945

Britain was in a poor economic state after the war. There was a large National Debt, war damage needed to be repaired, and unemployment, shortages and *inflation** all increased. The economy recovered steadily in the 1950s. This was partly due to the Marshall Plan (1948-52), by which the United States gave financial aid to western Europe, although the contribution Britain received was relatively small.

The Welfare State

The Labour party came to power in 1945, with the aim of rebuilding the economy and improving social conditions. The findings of the Beveridge report (1942) led to the establishment of the Welfare State, a system of social services organized and paid for by the government. The National Assurance Scheme was set up in 1946 to give financial help to the poor and elderly. The National Health Service followed in 1948, providing free medical care for all.

Nationalization

The Labour Party wanted Britain's major industries to be under public ownership. Between 1945 and 1951, 20% of British industries and services were nationalized, including water, gas, iron, coal, steel, electricity and the railways.

The railways were nationalized in 1948. This is a train from the period.

Education

After 1944 secondary modern schools were introduced, which provided a more technical education than grammar schools. In 1964 the Labour government introduced comprehensive schools. These were intended to replace grammar schools and secondary moderns, so that children of all abilities could be educated together. The minimum age for leaving school rose to 15 in 1949 and 16 in 1969.

The economy and industrial relations

The economy prospered until the early 1960s, when unemployment and inflation began to rise. Although the Conservative government gave financial help to the nationalized industries, the situation did not improve, and there was a series of major strikes in the late 1960s.

The *trade unions** resented attempts by both the Labour government (1964-70) and the Conservative government (1970-74) to their limit union power. In 1972 and 1974, there were serious miners' strikes, which led to power shortages. In 1974 the Conservatives introduced a three-day working week to try to save fuel, and the government fell from power as a result.

The new Labour government bargained with the unions. The unions agreed to moderate their pay claims in return for the introduction of laws in their favour. But when the economy did not improve, further wage restraints were imposed. This led to a series of strikes during the winter of 1978-79, which became known as the Winter of Discontent.

Old threepenny piece

Old penny

Old sixpence

In 1971 Britain adopted decimal currency.

Inflation increased rapidly and in May 1979 the Conservatives came to power, led by Margaret Thatcher, Britain's first woman Prime Minister. To save on public spending, they made economies in public services, particularly in education and the National Health Service, and closed unprofitable industries, including mines and dockyards. By 1983 unemployment was over three million. From the early 1980s the Conservatives passed laws to limit trade union power. They also followed a policy of *privatizing** many nationalized industries and services on the grounds that it would make them more profitable and efficient.

Race relations

The revival of the economy in the 1950s led to a shortage of labour. The government encouraged people from Commonwealth countries (see page 50), such as India, Pakistan, the West Indies and Cyprus, to come to work in Britain. Their presence caused widespread resentment, and immigrants were subject to discrimination over jobs and housing. In 1968 the Race Relations Act was passed to protect people from racial prejudice.

New political parties

In 1981 four Labour MPs left the moderate* wing of the Labour party to set up a new political party, the Social Democratic Party (SDP). It merged with the Liberals in 1988 to form the Social and Liberal Democratic Party (SLDP).

Ulster

In 1949 Eire declared itself a republic*. In the late 1960s discontent increased in Northern Ireland. Unemployment was high and the Catholics resented the Protestant majority in the Parliament at Stormont (see page 45). In 1968 trouble broke out between two rival organizations, the Irish Republican Army (IRA; a group of militant Catholic nationalists*) and the Ulster Volunteer Force (UVF: militant Protestants who did not want Ireland to be ruled separately from Great Britain). In 1969 Britain sent troops to Northern Ireland in an attempt to keep peace. But the violence continued. In 1970 a splinter group, the Provisional IRA, began a terrorist* campaign, demanding the removal of British troops from Ireland. In 1972 the Stormont Parliament was suspended and since then Northern Ireland has been governed from Westminster. Violence has continued into the 1990s.

Troops in Northern Ireland

International relations

After World War II relations between the former allies deteriorated. Two centres of power emerged: the USA and its allies in western Europe, and the USSR and its Communist* allies in eastern Europe. In 1949 the western allies set up the North Atlantic Treaty Organisation (NATO), by which they agreed to defend each other in case of attack. In response, the USSR and its allies formed the Warsaw Pact in 1955. The hostility without open conflict that existed between these two powers is known as the Cold War.

In 1962 the USSR established missile bases in Cuba, near America's coastline. However, the USSR withdrew these bases when America threatened war. This is known as the Cuban Missile Crisis.

Tension began to ease in the 1970s and since the mid-1980s both sides have been more willing to improve relations and to reduce nuclear arms.

The European Community

The European Economic Community (EEC), also called the Common Market, was set up in 1957 to promote and regulate trade between its members.

Flags of the EEC countries in 1957

Belgium   Italy   West Germany

Netherlands   Luxembourg   France

Britain was afraid EEC rules would restrict British trade with the Commonwealth and did not join until 1973. Now called the European Community (EC), the organization plans to create closer monetary and political links between its members. In 1982 it set up a system called the ERM (Exchange Rate Mechanism) which controls the exchange rate of European currencies. Britain joined the ERM in 1990.

Decolonization

Between 1947 and 1975 most European *colonies** became independent. Weakened by the war, the colonial powers could no longer afford to keep armies abroad. Public opinion was also changing; it was no longer considered acceptable for one country to rule another. In 1947 India became the first country to gain independence, after a campaign by the Congress Party,

Mahatma Gandhi

led by Mahatma Gandhi. To try to avoid religious clashes, Britain split India into two states: India (mainly *Hindu**) and Pakistan (mainly *Muslim**).

Between 1957 (Ghana) and 1968 (Swaziland) all African countries except Rhodesia (see below) became independent. Most of the former colonies have remained in a loose association with Britain called the Commonwealth.

Colonial wars and other conflicts

Decolonization often involved war, both against colonial powers and internally, to decide who should come to power.

In Palestine tension had grown since 1917, Britain declared itself in favour of creating a national home there for the Jewish people. This became known as the Balfour Declaration, after the Foreign Secretary, Arthur Balfour. In 1920 the country came under British control. In the 1920s and 1930s many Jews settled in Palestine to escape persecution in parts of Europe. Tension between native Arabs and Jewish immigrants led to war in 1946. The British withdrew in 1948, and the Jewish state of Israel was created within Palestine. Arab resentment of subsequent Israeli expansion is the root of many current problems in the Middle East.

The Israeli flag

In 1956 the Egyptian government nationalized the Suez Canal without consulting the British and the French, who were major shareholders. They sent troops to Egypt to protect their interests, but international pressure forced them to withdraw. This is known as the Suez Crisis.

There was also *terrorist** warfare against British rule in Kenya (1948-54), Malaya (1950-53) and Cyprus (1955-59). In Rhodesia a white minority broke away under *UDI** in 1965. This led to civil war. In 1980 Rhodesia became independent as Zimbabwe under a *black majority government**.

This bird is Zimbabwe's emblem of independence.

In 1982 Argentina invaded the Falkland Islands, one of Britain's few remaining colonies. Britain sent troops to fight, and Argentina surrendered after ten weeks.

In 1990 Iraq invaded Kuwait. In January 1991, with the consent of the *United Nations**, several countries, including Britain sent troops to the Gulf to force the Iraqis out. Iraq withdrew in March 1991.

Key dates

1946-48 Welfare State is set up.

1947 India becomes independent.

1949 Eire declares itself a republic.

1952 Accession of Queen Elizabeth II

1956 Suez Crisis

1965 The death penalty is abolished.

1968 Race Relations Act

1970 Oil is discovered in the North Sea.

1973 Britain joins the EEC.

1978-79 The Winter of Discontent

1981 Unemployment riots in Liverpool, Birmingham and London

1982 War with Argentina over Britain's sovereignty of the Falkland Islands

1991 War with Iraq

Who is who in the arts

This list contains brief details of the lives and achievements of some of the most important artistic and literary figures in British history.

Austen, Jane (1775-1817).   Novelist. Most of her novels portray life in provincial England. They include *Emma*, *Pride and Prejudice*, and *Sense and Sensibility*.

Adam, Robert (1728-92).   Architect. He introduced an architectural style into Britain that was heavily influenced by the styles of ancient Greece and Rome.

Bede (c.673-735).   Historian and theologian. He lived most of his life as a monk. In 731 he completed the first known history of Britain, called *The Ecclesiastical History of the English People*. His other books include religious and scientific works.

Blake, William (1757-1827).   Poet and artist. His poems often express his radical religious and political ideas. They include a collection called *Songs of Innocence and Songs of Experience*. He illustrated many of his own works.

Bronte.   Family of authors. The three sisters, **Charlotte** (1816-55), **Emily** (1818-48), and **Anne** (1820-49) Bronte wrote novels, most of them based on life in rural Yorkshire. The best known are Charlotte's *Jane Eyre*, Emily's *Wuthering Heights* and Anne's *The Tenant of Wildfell Hall*.

Brown, Capability (1716-83).   Landscape gardener. He broke away from the formal garden design that was popular in England at that time. Instead he introduced a freer, more natural style. He designed gardens at Warwick Castle and Blenheim Palace.

Britten, Benjamin (1913-1976).   Composer. He wrote orchestral and church music, but is probably most famous for his operas. These include *Peter Grimes*, *Billy Budd* and *The Turn of the Screw*.

Burns, Robert (1759-96).   Scottish poet. He was famous for writing in Scottish dialect when poetry was usually written in more formal language. His work includes *Holy Willie's Prayer*, *To a Mouse* and *Tam O'Shanter*.

Byrd, William (1543-1623).   Composer. He was organist at Lincoln Cathedral, then later, with another composer, Thomas Tallis (1505-85), honorary organist to Elizabeth I. One of Byrd's most famous collections of church music, *Cantiones Sacrae*, was dedicated to the Queen.

Byron, Lord George Gordon (1788-1824). Poet. He travelled widely, settling in in Italy in 1816 and Greece in 1823. His most famous poems include *Don Juan* and *Childe Harold's Pilgrimage*.

Chaucer, Geoffrey (c.1340-1400).   Poet. One of the most important medieval poets, he was influenced by French and Italian literature. He is most famous for *The Canterbury Tales* c.1387.

Christie, Agatha (1890-1976).   Novelist. She was famous for detective novels. Her best-known character, Hercule Poirot, was introduced in her first novel, *The Mysterious Affair at Styles*.

Constable, John (1776-1837).   Landscape painter. He was born in Sussex and often painted there, depicting the same view in different weather or light conditions. His paintings include *The Hay Wain* and *Salisbury Cathedral*.

Dickens, Charles (1812-70).   Novelist. His novels comment on poverty and social injustice, especially towards children. Among his best known works are *Oliver Twist*, *Nicholas Nickleby* and *David Copperfield*.

Donne, John (1571-1631).   Poet. From 1621 he was Dean of St. Paul's Church in London, where he was famous for his sermons. Many of his poems are best known by their first lines such as 'No man is an island' and 'Death, be not proud'.

Doyle, Sir Arthur Conan (1859-1930). Novelist. He is most famous for creating the investigator Sherlock Holmes, who appeared in over 60 stories.

Elgar, Sir Edward (1857-1934). Composer. He wrote both choral and orchestral music. One of his most successful works was the *Enigma Variations* (1899); other works include *Sea Pictures* and *The Dream of Gerontius*.

Eliot, George (1819-1880).   Novelist. Born Mary Ann Evans, she wrote under a male pseudonym. Her portrayals of rural Victorian society often criticize its hypocrisies and injustices. Her books include *The Mill on the Floss*, *Silas Marner* and *Middlemarch*.

Gainsborough, Thomas (1727-88).   Artist. He mainly painted landscapes and portraits of well-known people. Before Gainsborough, English artists painted imaginary rather than real landscapes.

Golding, William (1911-).   Novelist. Many of his books concern people's reactions to new or strange situations. They include *Lord of the Flies*, *The Spire* and *Rites of Passage*.

Greene, Graham (1904-91).   Novelist. Many of his books deal with religious issues and people's commitment to causes or ideals. They include *Brighton Rock*, *The Power and the Glory* and *The Third Man*.

Hepworth, Barbara (1903-1975). Sculptor. Much of her early work consists of human figures in wood or marble. Her later sculptures are more abstract, often influenced by the landscape of Cornwall, where she lived much of her life.

Hogarth, William (1697-1764).   Artist and engraver. Much of his work is witty and sarcastic, criticizing or ridiculing social conditions or manners.

Johnson, Samuel (1709-84). Lexicographer, essayist, poet and critic. He wrote the first dictionary of the English language, published in 1755.

Jones, Inigo (1573-c.1652).   Architect. He was influenced by the Italian architect Palladio. His buildings include the Queen's House at Greenwich and the Banqueting Hall in Whitehall, London.

Jonson, Ben (1572-1637).   Playwright. He wrote comic plays, often ridiculing aspects of political life. These include *Every Man in his Humour*, *The Alchemist* and *Bartholomew Fayre*.

Joyce, James (1882-1941).   Irish writer. Much of his work attempts to find new forms of expression: *Ulysses* contains new types of narrative, and *Finnegan's Wake* is written in a complex, dream-like language.

Keats, John (1795-1821).   Poet. He trained as a doctor but gave up medicine to write poetry. Many of his poems contain vivid descriptions of sensations and emotions. His most famous works include *Hyperion*, *Ode to a Nightingale* and *The Eve of St. Agnes*.

Langland, William (c.1332-c.1400).   Poet. He wrote *The Vision concerning Piers Plowman*, which condemns the social and moral evils of 14th-century England.

Lawrence, D. H. (1885-1930).   Novelist and poet. He was the son of a miner and became a teacher. Some of his most famous works include *Sons and Lovers*, *The Rainbow* and *Lady Chatterley's Lover*.

Lely, Peter (1616-80).   Anglo-German portrait painter. He worked for Charles I, Cromwell and Charles II. His most famous paintings are portraits of women at the court of Charles II.

Marlowe, Christopher (1564-93). Playwright. He wrote both comedies and tragedies, and influenced Shakespeare and many others. His most famous works include *The Tragicall History of Doctor Faustus*, *Tamburlaine the Great*, *The Jew of Malta* and *Edward II*.

Marvell, Andrew (1621-1678).   Poet. A Puritan and republican, he worked for Oliver Cromwell and was an assistant to John Milton. His poems include *To his Coy Mistress* and *A Garden*.

Millais, John Everett (1829-96).   Artist. In 1848 he set up an artistic group, the Pre-Raphaelite Brotherhood, with the painters Dante Gabriel Rossetti and William Holman Hunt. They concentrated on religious and literary subjects, depicted in a clear, detailed style.

Milton, John (1608-74).   Poet. He became a Puritan in his middle age and wrote many tracts in support of the Puritan cause. His most famous works include *Samson Agonistes*, *Paradise Lost* and *Paradise Regained*.

Moore, Henry (1898-1986).   Sculptor. Many of his works were huge and monumental, and were made to be placed outdoors. Though abstract, they are based on objects found in nature, like the human body or rock formations.

Morris, William (1834-96).   Poet and artist. He was a friend of Millais and the Pre-Raphaelites. He objected to increasing industrialization and founded the Arts and Crafts movement which promoted hand-crafted workmanship.

Nash, John (1752-1835).   Architect. He laid out Regent's Park in London and designed many houses and streets. In 1815 he designed the Royal Pavilion at Brighton for the Prince Regent (who later became George IV).

Olivier, Laurence (1907-1990).   Actor. He first became famous for his appearances in Shakespeare's plays, especially Henry V and Hamlet. Later he also worked as a film director, appearing in his own critically acclaimed versions of *Hamlet* and *Richard III*.

Pepys, Samuel (1633-1703). Diarist. From 1660 to 1669 he wrote a detailed diary about London life. It includes such events as the Plague and the Fire of London.

Purcell, Henry (1659-95). Composer. He was composer to the court and wrote many pieces for both Church and State occasions. The opera *Dido and Aeneas* (1689) one of his most important works, is still frequently performed.

Reynolds, Joshua (1723-92). Portrait painter. He was the first president of the Royal Academy (founded in 1768 by George III to encourage art and architecture). His paintings include *A Portrait of Miss Bowles with her Dog.*

Scott, Sir Walter (1771-1832). Scottish novelist and poet. His collection of poems, *Minstrelsy of the Scottish Border*, was published in 1802. Later in his career he wrote historical novels such as *Waverley*, *Rob Roy* and *Ivanhoe*.

Shakespeare, William (1564-1616). Playwright. He was born in Stratford-Upon-Avon, but left to work in London. He wrote tragic, comic and historical plays which include *Othello*, *The Taming of the Shrew*, and *Henry V*. He also wrote a series of love poems called sonnets.

Shaw, George Bernard (1856-1950). Irish Playwright and critic. Many of his writings deal with political and social injustices. His plays include *Pygmalion*, *Mrs Warren's Profession* and *Saint Joan.*

Shelley, Percy Bysshe (1792-1822). Poet. He was educated at Oxford and later settled in Italy, where he died. Among his most famous works are *The Skylark*, *Adonais*, and *Prometheus Unbound*. His second wife Mary Wollstonecraft Shelley (1797-1851), wrote *Frankenstein.*

Sheridan, Richard Brinsley (1751-1816). Anglo-Irish playwright. He became famous for his comedies, including *The Rivals* and *The School for Scandal*. His plays often make fun of the social conventions of the day.

Sitwell, Edith (1887-1964). Poet. She came from a literary family, and first became famous for *Façade*, a series of poems inspired by dance rhythms. Later works include *The Little Ghost who Died for Love* and *Gold Coast Customs.*

Sullivan, Arthur (1842-1900). Composer. With the dramatist W.S. Gilbert (1836-1911) he wrote wrote light comic operas such as *HMS Pinafore* and *The Mikado.*

Turner, Joseph Mallord William (1775-1851). Artist. He experimented with different techniques to create new light and colour effects. Among his most famous works are *Rain, Steam and Speed*, *The Fighting Temeraire* and paintings of Venice.

Walton, William (1902-83). Composer. He wrote choral and orchestral music, including several film scores. His most famous works include *Façade* (a setting of Edith Sitwell's poems) and *Belshazzar's Feast.*

Wilde, Oscar (1854-1900). Irish author and playwright. His works include the novel *The Portrait of Dorian Grey*, the comedies *Lady Windermere's Fan* and *The Importance of Being Earnest*, and many essays, poems and short stories.

Wodehouse, P. G. (1818-1975). Novelist. His most famous characters are Bertie Wooster and his butler Jeeves, who appear in several comic novels. He also collaborated on the lyrics of musicals by Jerome Kern, George Gershwin and others.

Woolf, Virginia (1882-1942). Novelist and critic. Her books include *Mrs Dalloway*, *Orlando* and *To the Lighthouse.*

Wordsworth, William (1770-1850). Poet. Much of his poetry was inspired by the power of nature and the simplicity of rural life. His most famous works include *The Prelude*, *Daffodils* and *Intimations of Mortality.*

Wren, Christopher (1632-1723). Architect. He first studied mathematics, and later was professor of astronomy at Oxford. In 1666 he drew up plans to rebuild London after the Great Fire. His most famous building is St Paul's Cathedral; others include the Sheldonian Theatre, Oxford.

Yeats, William Butler (1865-1939). Irish Poet and playwright. He based some of his work on Irish myths and legends, and helped to revive an interest in Irish literature and the Gaelic language. His poems include *Byzantium*, *The Wild Swans at Coole* and *The Salley Gardens.*

Glossary

This glossary contains words used elsewhere in the book which may be unfamiliar. Words related to the heading appear in **bold** within the text of the entry. If a word appears in italic type followed by an asterisk, like this, *charter*, it has its own entry in the glossary.

Abdicate. To give up the throne.

Angles. A people from northern Germany, many of whom settled in the north and east of England in the 5th and 6th centuries.

Annex. To add or join a piece of land to a larger territory either by conquest or political agreement.

Armistice. A pact made by warring countries to suspend fighting and discuss peace.

Balance of power. A situation in which no nation or group of nations is stronger than its opponents.

Barbarian. The name given by the Romans to anybody living outside their empire who did not follow a Roman way of life.

Baron. In the Middle Ages, a landowning nobleman.

Black majority government. A government brought to power by an electorate with a majority of black voters. This is in contrast with a **white minority government**, which is elected by a minority of the population which happens to be white.

Borough. A town with a corporation conferred by royal *charter*. From the 13th century each borough sent two representatives to Parliament. In the 18th century boroughs where local landowners influenced the choice of MP were known as **Pocket boroughs**. Boroughs where few people lived but which still sent two MPs to Parliament were known as **Rotten boroughs**. Most corrupt boroughs were abolished in 1832.

Boycott. To refuse to have dealings (especially financial or diplomatic) with someone or something.

Bubonic plague. A deadly disease that causes fever and swellings called **buboes**.

Celts. A people first in evidence in central Europe after 1000BC. The Celts first came to Britain in about 500BC.

Charter. A formal document by which the monarch gives certain rights and privileges to his subjects. Charters were granted to create *boroughs* or other corporations such as guilds, or later, trading companies.

Christianity. A religion which originated in Palestine. It evolved from the teachings of a man called Jesus of Nazareth. His followers, known as **Christians**, called him the **Christ**, Greek for 'Son of God'.

Coalition. A government formed by an alliance of political parties, usually in times of crisis such as war.

Colony. An overseas subject territory or a group of people, known as **colonists**, who settle in a territory far from their homeland.

Communist. A believer in a political ideology called **Communism** based on the theories of Karl Marx. Marx believed that society should be based on common ownership. In 1917 the Russian empire (later known as the Soviet Union) became the first Communist state. After World War II all eastern European countries under Soviet influence became Communist.

Crusades. A series of military expeditions undertaken between the 11th and 15th centuries by *Christian* European powers. The original aim was to recapture Palestine (known as the Holy Land) from *Muslim* Turks.

Customs and excise duties. Customs duties are taxes on imported goods paid by the importer. Excise duties are taxes on imported goods paid by the consumer.

Democracy. Government by the people or their elected representatives. A democracy is characterized by recognition of equality of rights and privileges for all.

Depose. To remove a ruler from the throne.

Dominion. A self-governing *colony* associated with the country that founded it, but not ruled by it.

Dues. A general term used to describe the money, rents and services that had to be paid by a man to his feudal lord.

Duty. See *Customs and excise duties*.

East India Trading Company. An English commercial company established in 1600. It had a *monopoly* of trade between England and the Far East. Before 1784 it controlled large parts of India.

Excommunication. A declaration made by the Pope, expelling an individual from the Roman Catholic Church. A person who has been **excommunicated** is no longer allowed to take part in Church ceremony or ritual.

Excise Duty. See *Customs and excise duties*.

Fiefs. Land given by the monarch to nobles or high-ranking Churchmen in return for *dues*.

Heresy. A belief contrary to the accepted teaching of a particular church. A person holding such beliefs is known as a **heretic**.

Highlands. In Britain, the mountainous region in northern Scotland; its inhabitants are known as **Highlanders**.

Hindu. A follower of **Hinduism**, a religion which originated in India. Hindus worship many deities and believe in reincarnation.

Home Rule. A slogan of the Irish *nationalist** movement between 1870 and 1914. Its followers wanted the Act of Union (1801) to be repealed, and Ireland to have its own Parliament within the framework of the British empire.

Impeachment. A statement made in the presence of judges in the House of Lords, charging a high ranking officer with serious offences.

Independents. A Protestant group whose members insisted that every congregation should govern itself, independently of a central church authority.

Inflation. A general rise in prices caused by an excess in demand over supply of goods or by an increase in the supply of money.

Interdict. A declaration made by the Pope forbidding the practice of certain rituals and ceremonies of the Roman Catholic Church.

Interest. A fee charged for borrowing money, usually on a percentage basis.

Jacobite. A supporter of the Stuart line of kings descended from James II who was deposed in 1688. The word comes from *Jacobus*, the Latin form of the name James.

Jutes. A Germanic people who originated in Jutland in Denmark. They occupied Kent in about AD450.

Lowlander. An inhabitant of the lowland areas in the south of Scotland.

Majority government. A government which has more MPs elected to the House of Commons than all the other parties put together. A government has a **working majority** when it has just enough supporters to ensure that its policies are always carried through Parliament.

Minority. Below the age of majority (adulthood). When the monarch is a child (a **minor**), a *regent** rules on his or her behalf.

Minority government. A government whose party has fewer MPs than the opposition parties put together. It survives because the opposition parties are more opposed to each other than to the government and therefore fail to unite together against it.

Miracle. An event for which there is no rational explanation and which is deemed to be an intervention by God.

Mobilize. To prepare or move an army into position before declaring war.

Mogul empire. An empire in India founded in the 14th century by the Mogul dynasty (family). It began in the north and eventually covered most of India. In the early 18th century, it started to decline; the last Mogul emperor was deposed by the English in 1857.

Monopoly. In the 16th and 17th centuries, the name for the exclusive right, granted by the monarch, to trade in a particular commodity or area, without other competition.

Muslim. A follower of Islam, the religion founded in Mecca, Arabia, by the prophet Muhammad.

Nationalists. People who believe in and campaign for their country's right to remain independent of other countries.

Neutral. Impartial. A neutral country refuses to help or support either of two opposing sides. According to international law, feuding countries may not involve neutral countries in their struggles.

Outlaw. Someone deprived of the protection of the law, usually a criminal.

Overlord. A supreme lord or master, usually the king. However, in some situations a king could be the overlord of another King in another country.

Pagan. A word originally used by *Christians** to describe someone who was not a Christian and worshipped non-Christian gods.

Patent. A document signed by the monarch which gives an inventor the right, for a set period of time, to make exclusive use of his invention. In return the inventor must publish information on his invention or discovery.

Peerage. The aristocracy or nobility; a **peer** is a nobleman.

Picts. A Roman name for the people living in the area north of the River Forth.

Pocket borough. See *Borough**.

Poll tax. A tax first imposed in 1222 on every person in the country over the age of 14.

Presbyterianism. The official church in Scotland. A form of Protestantism based on the ideas of John Calvin, a 16th century Church reformer. There are no compulsory rites, rituals or other forms of worship.

Pressure group. Any group set up to lobby the Government over political issues.

Privatize. To turn a nationalized industry into a private company by selling shares in it to private investors.

Radical. A term first used in the 18th century to describe anyone advocating fundamental political or social reform.

Regent. Someone, usually a relative, who rules on behalf of the monarch if he or she is unable to do so. Regents are appointed mainly when the monarch is too young to rule, as in the case of Henry VI; or too ill, like George III.

Religious freedom. An individual's freedom to follow whatever religion he or she chooses.

Republic. A state or country without a king, queen or emperor, governed by elected representatives or an elected president.

Rotten borough. See *Borough**

Royal domain. The territory of a monarch over which he has authority.

Saxons. A group of north German people who conquered most of Britain in the 5th and 6th centuries.

Serf. Another word for *villein**.

Shire. A unit of local government in Anglo-Saxon Britain. The Normans called shires 'counties'.

Smelting. The process by which heat is used to extract metal from rock or sediment.

Smuggling. The illegal import or export of goods without paying *customs duties**.

Sovereign. A monarch or other ruler who holds supreme authority (or **sovereignty**). A **sovereign state** is independent of outside authority.

Stalemate. A situation in which no progress is made. The term is often used to describe a war or battle that no one is winning.

Subsidy. A parliamentary grant of money.

Terrorist. Someone who takes part in an organized system of terror and intimidation for political purposes.

Tories. A nickname given in the 17th century to the Court Party. (The word was originally slang for 'Irish robbers'; many members of the Court Party were Anglo-Irish landowners.) After 1834 the Tory Party began to be called the Conservative Party.

Trade union. An organization of workers within a trade or industry which undertakes collective bargaining with employers on behalf of its members, in order to protect their interests. The first trade unions were established in the late 18th century.

Treason. The crime of betraying the government or monarch. In Britain, treason is still punishable by death.

Trial by combat. Before the law reforms of Henry II, a person's innocence or guilt was often tested by means of a fight with his accuser.

Tribute. A payment, in money or services, made by a subject to a ruler or by a ruler to another ruler as an acknowledgement of submission.

UDI. The Unilateral Declaration of Independence made in 1965 by a **white minority government** (the Rhodesian Front) in the British *colony** of Rhodesia.

Ulster. The former kingdom in the north of Ireland that was *annexed** by England in 1461. It was *colonized** by the English and the Scots from the mid-17th century. In 1921 the British government divided Ireland into Northern Ireland (which was still ruled by Britain) and Southern Ireland (which was granted *Home Rule**). In the process, Ulster was split between these two new areas.

United Nations. (UN). An association of states set up in 1945 to promote international peace and co-operation.

Veto. To withold consent for a proposed measure.

Villein. A medieval peasant who paid *dues** and worked on his lord's land in return for land of his own. Villeins could not leave the lord's manor without his consent.

Vows. Promises made by monks and nuns to abide by the rules of their religious order. These vows usually include those of poverty, chastity and obedience.

Whig. A nickname, applied in the 17th century to the Country Party. (The term originally meant 'Scottish horse thieves'.)

Advances in science and technology

1477 *Dictes and Sayenges of the Phylosophers*, the first book to be printed in England, is produced by William Caxton.

1662 The Royal Society, Britain's first scientific society, is founded.

1665-66 Isaac Newton establishes laws of light and motion and formulates the law of gravity.

1675 The first astronomical observatory in Britain is built at Greenwich.

1681 Street lights (oil-powered) are put up in London for the first time.

1698 Thomas Savery invents the first steam pump, the precursor of the steam engine.

c.1750-1900 The Industrial Revolution (*see pages* 34-35)

1774 Joseph Priestley discovers oxygen. Further research based on his discovery forms the basis of modern ideas about how chemical elements combine to create compounds.

1785 First crossing of the English Channel by hot-air balloon.

1792 William Murdoch is the first person to use coal gas to light a house. For domestic purposes it is later superseded by natural gas.

1796 Edward Jenner innoculates a young boy with a cowpox virus, successfully making him immune to smallpox.

1808 John Dalton's atomic theory is published. He is the first person to gather evidence that matter is made up of tiny particles called atoms.

1827 John McAdam, Surveyor of Roads, starts to build roads out of broken granite instead of stone or dirt. This revolutionizes transport, making roads more durable and travel easier.

1831 Michael Faraday discovers electromagnetic induction, the basis of electric motors, dynamos and generators.

1834 Charles Babbage designs an 'analytical machine' which is able to make calculations and store the results. Although it is never built, it uses many principles on which modern digital computers are based.

1830-50 Medical advances (*see page* 38)

1851 The first underwater cable, used for transmitting telegraph messages, is laid under the Channel betwen Dover, England and Cap Gris Nez, France.

1856 William Perkins makes the first chemical dye (mauve) and starts the first chemical dye industry in Britain.

1839 Henry Fox-Talbot invents light sensitive photographic paper.

1859 Charles Darwin proposes a theory of evolution in his book, *The Origin of the Species*.

1878 Electric street lighting is installed in London; Britain's first telephone company is set up.

1899 The first motor buses appear in London; the world's first underground railway line opens in London; radio signals are sent for the first time from England to France.

1901 Gugliemo Marconi, an Italian working in London, sends the first wireless signal across the Atlantic using morse code.

1903 *The Great Train Robbery* is the first film to be shown commercially in London.

1906 Frederick Hopkins identifies vitamins. His discovery leads to the cure and prevention of diseases caused by vitamin deficiencies.

1911 Ernest Rutherford, a New Zealander working in Cambridge, discovers the nuclear properties of the atom. His work forms the basis of nuclear science.

1919 The Englishmen J.W. Alcock and A.W. Brown make the first flight across the Atlantic.

1924 John Logie Baird demonstrates the principles of television and transmits the first moving pictures.

1928 From the fungus *penicillium*, Sir Alexander Fleming develops penicillin, which prevents the growth of certain bacteria. Many illnesses are now cured using antibiotics, drugs derived from similar sources.

1930 Acrylic plastic is invented.

mid-1930s Robert Watson-Watt develops a long range radar system which can track advancing aircraft within 40 miles.

1937 Frank Whittle invents the first jet engine. It is smaller and lighter than earlier engines, and means that aeroplanes no longer need propellers. Most aeroplanes now use jet engines.

1936 The world's first television service is set up in London.

1948 The first electronic computer, Mark 1, is built in Manchester, England.

1959 Charles Cockerell invents the hovercraft.

1961 The Hawker Siddley Harrier, the first aeroplane able to take off vertically, flies for the first time.

1968 England and France build Concorde, the first aeroplane able to travel faster than the speed of sound.

1978 The first baby is born using *in vitro* fertilization, a means of fertilizing human eggs outside the body and then placing them in the womb.

1987 Britain and France start to build a tunnel under the English Channel — one of the longest tunnels to be built under water.

British monarchs and Prime Ministers

This list contains the names of English, Scottish and Welsh rulers from the ninth century to the present day. The section headings show each monarch's country of origin, or, for later rulers, the name of his or her family or 'house'.

Saxon kings

Egbert	802-39
Ethelwulf	839-58
Ethelbald	858-60
Ethelbert	860-65
Ethelred I	865-71
Alfred the Great	871-99
Edward the Elder	899-924
Athelstan	924-39
Edmund	939-46
Edred	946-55
Edwy	955-59
Edgar	959-75
Edward the Martyr	975-78
Ethelred II (the Unready)	978-1016
Edmund Ironside	1016

Danish kings

Cnut	1016-35
Harold I Harefoot	1035-40
Harthacnut	1040-42

Saxon kings

Edward the Confessor	1042-66
Harold II	1066

Norman kings

William the Conqueror	1066-87
William II	1087-1100
Henry I	1100-35
Stephen	1135-54

House of Plantagenets

Henry II	1154-89
Richard I	1189-99
John	1199-1216
Henry III	1216-72
Edward I	1272-1307
Edward II	1307-27
Edward III	1327-77
Richard II	1377-99

House of Lancaster

Henry IV	1399-1413
Henry V	1413-22
Henry VI	1422-61

House of York

Edward IV	1461-83
Edward V	1483
Richard III	1483-85

House of Tudor

Henry VII	1485-1509
Henry VIII	1509-47
Edward VI	1547-53
Mary I	1553-58
Elizabeth I	1558-1603

House of Stuart

James I	1603-25
Charles I	1625-49

The Commonwealth

Between 1649 and 1660 the monarchy was abolished in Britain. The country became a *republic** and was ruled by a Lord Protector and his council. The Lord Protectors were:

Oliver Cromwell	1649-59
Richard Cromwell	1659-60

House of Stuart (restored)

Charles II	1660-85
James II	1685-88
William III with	1688-1702
Mary II	1688-94
Anne	1702-14

House of Hanover

George I	1714-27
George II	1727-60
George III	1760-1820
George IV	1820-30
William IV	1830-37

House of Saxe-Coburg-Gotha

(This was the family name of Queen Victoria's German husband, Prince Albert. It remained the name of the royal family until 1917 when it was changed to Windsor).

Victoria	1837-1901
Edward VII	1901-10

House of Windsor

George V	1910-36
Edward VIII	1936
George VI	1936-52
Elizabeth II	1952-

Scottish monarchs

Kenneth MacAlpin (839-60), Donald I (860-62), Constantine I (862-77), Aedh (877-78), Eocha (878-89), Donald II (889-900), Constantine II (900-42), Malcolm I (942-54), Indulf (954-962), Dubh (962-966), Cuilean (966-71), Kenneth II (971-95), Constantine III (995-97), Kenneth III (997-1005), Malcolm II (1005-1034), Duncan I (1034-40), Macbeth (1040-57), Malcolm III, known as Canmore (1058-93), Donald Bane (1093-94), Duncan II (1094), Donald Bane (restored 1094-97), Edgar (1097-1107), Alexander I (1107-24), David I (1124-53), Malcolm IV (1153-65), William the Lion (1165-1214), Alexander II (1214-49), Alexander III (1249-86), Margaret of Norway (1286-90), monarchy in dispute (1290-92), John Balliol (1292-96), monarchy in dispute (1296-1306), Robert I the Bruce (1306-29), David II (1329-71), Robert II (1371-90), Robert III (1390-1406), James I (1406-37), James II (1437-60), James III (1460-88), James IV (1488-1513), James V (1513-42), Mary (1542-67), James VI* (1567-1625)

Princes of Wales

Rhodri (844-78), Anarawd (878-916), Idwal (916-42), Hywel the Good (942-950), Iago (950-79), Hywel the Bad (979-85), Cadwallon (985-86), Maredudd (986-99), Cynan (999-1005), Llywelyn Seisyll (1018-23), Iago (1023-1039), Gruffydd Llwelyn (1039-63), Bleddyn (1063-75), Gruffydd Rhys (1081-1137), Owain (1137-70), Dafydd (1170-94), Llwelyn the Great (1194-1240), David (1240-46), Llwelyn Gruffydd (1246-82)

Prime Ministers of England

W=Whig T=Tory Cln=Coalition P=Peelite L=Liberal C=Conservative Lab=Labour

Name	Party	Years	Name	Party	Years
Robert Walpole	W	1721-42	William Gladstone	L	1868-74
Earl of Wilmington	W	1742-43	Benjamin Disraeli	C	1874-80
Henry Pelham	W	1743-54	William Gladstone	L	1880-85
Duke of Newcastle	W	1754-56	Marquess of Salisbury	C	1885-86
Duke of Devonshire	W	1756-57	William Gladstone	L	1886
Earl of Bute	T	1762-63	Marquess of Salisbury	C	1886-92
George Grenville	W	1763-65	William Gladstone	L	1892-94
Marquess of Rockingham	W	1782	Earl of Rosebery	L	1894-95
Earl of Shelburne	W	1782-83	Marquess of Salisbury	C	1895-1902
Duke of Portland	Cln	1783	Arthur Balfour	C	1902-05
William Pitt the Younger	T	1783-1801	Henry Campbell-Bannerman	L	1905-08
Henry Addington	T	1801-04	Herbert Asquith	L	1908-15
William Pitt the Younger	T	1804-06	Herbert Asquith	Cln	1915-16
Lord Grenville	W	1806-07	David Lloyd George	Cln	1916-22
Duke of Portland	T	1807-09	Andrew Bonar Law	C	1922-23
Spencer Perceval	T	1809-12	James Ramsay MacDonald	Lab	1924
Earl of Liverpool	T	1812-27	Stanley Baldwin	C	1924-29
George Canning	T	1827	James Ramsay MacDonald	Lab	1929-31
Viscount Goderich	T	1827-28	James Ramsay MacDonald	Cln	1931-35
Duke of Wellington	T	1828-30	Stanley Baldwin	Cln	1935-37
Earl Grey	W	1830-34	Neville Chamberlain	Cln	1937-40
Viscount Melbourne	W	1834	Winston Churchill	Cln	1940-45
Robert Peel	T	1834-35	Winston Churchill	C	1945
Viscount Melbourne	W	1835-41	Clement Attlee	Lab	1945-51
Robert Peel	T	1841-46	Winston Churchill	C	1951-55
Lord John Russell	W	1846-52	Anthony Eden	C	1955-57
Earl of Derby	T	1852	Harold Macmillan	C	1957-63
Earl of Aberdeen	P	1852-55	Alec Douglas-Home	C	1963-64
Viscount Palmerston	L	1855-58	Harold Wilson	Lab	1964-70
Earl of Derby	C	1858-59	Edward Heath	C	1970-74
Viscount Palmerston	L	1859-65	Harold Wilson	Lab	1974-76
Earl Russell	L	1865-66	James Callaghan	Lab	1976-79
Earl of Derby	C	1866-68	Margaret Thatcher	C	1979-90
Benjamin Disraeli	C	1868	John Major	C	1990-

*In 1603 James VI was crowned James I of England. After this both countries were ruled by the same monarch.

Index

This index will refer you to names and subjects in the main part of the book. Some people, however, only appear in the reference section, and not in the index: for artistic and literary figures see the 'Who's who' on pages 51-53.

First published in 1991 by Usborne Publishing Ltd, 83-85 Saffron Hill,
London EC1N 8RT, England.